DIMN VORE TRATEM

Focused

A guide to unlocking your potential

Contents

Prologue

I have written this book with the intention to inspire people to think, to learn, to create, to explore, and to propel humanity to the next steps in evolution. I have written this for the people who question why and how, and desire to find answers to those questions. I have written this book with the hopes that it will stimulate your mind and encourage you to think.

I do not hold my views to be absolute, I speak from my current level of understanding, I know that reality is subjective. I simply search for my subjective truth and any objective truths. I encourage you to think, to learn, to question, to investigate and to come to your own conclusions.

I believe that working to master the mind will lead humanity to the next frontier. I believe we have access to nearly infinite information and power, but we must unlock our full potential. If you believe you are capable of more, I encourage you to explore the power of the mind. This book is a guide that may propel you towards the next steps of human evolution. This book will discuss some of the fundamental laws and workings of the universe.

I will not simply speak of theories. I will provide practical tips and share knowledge that can possibly alter the course of your life as it has altered mine.

I believe that the path to peace, wealth, prosperity, and happiness is very simple, the key is to be true to yourself, and be willing to make the changes required to achieve the goals that you seek.

I have tried to make this book as simple and concise as possible, in hopes of reaching the greatest number of people and communicating in a way that can be understood easily. In this book I use may, can, should and other similar adjectives frequently because I understand the dangers of using absolutes. For the sake of simplicity, and not wasting your time with pointless words or details, some of the transitions between topics and paragraphs may not be smooth. Yet I believe using 100 words to explain something that can be adequately explained in 10 words is illogical and ineffective.

This book is written under an alias, so if this book has been referred to you it will be due to the quality of its contents.

1

Mindset

Your mindset dictates your inner reality. Once your mindset changes your outer reality will change to match it.

Mindsets are essential to the way humans think and how they operate. Changing and evolving your mindset is one of the quickest ways to change your circumstances. Different mindsets, lead to different thoughts, which lead to different actions and habits, which lead to different results. One of the quickest ways to grow and evolve is to change your mindset. If you want a new outcome in your life, different than your current situation consider changing your mindset. Wealthy people think like wealthy people, happy people have mindsets that lead to happiness. People with similar mindsets tend to live similar lives, because your outer reality is a symptom of your thoughts and that is a symptom of your mindset. Some people believe who they are can't change, but your current situation is a result of your current way of thinking. Many people want to change their life but fail to see the connection between their mindset(s) and their life.

If you have a mindset that you want to do as little work and possible, and the life you want to live requires years of hard work, your mindset is in direct contradiction of the reality you wish to create, and it is unlikely you will achieve it, while maintaining that mindset. If you pursue two opposing things your mind will have to fight against itself. A split *focus* is not an effective means of operation, and antithetical[1] aims may be the least effective form of operation. Another example of antithetical operation that plagues humanity is emotions being opposed to logic. If your logic and reasoning are opposed to your feelings and emotions there is a flaw in one or both. This phenomena leads to different regions of the brain constantly fighting against each other. Your mindset(s) shape your thoughts and beliefs, and your thoughts and beliefs shape your emotions. Mindset(s) that are illogical or impractical lead to this dilemma. With illogical mindset(s) it is nearly impossible to make sense of your reality, and the mind innately craves to understand reality.

The evolutionary method humans have developed to better understand reality is logic and reasoning. So when your mindsets contradicts logic or reality, your mind will crave exactly what you refuse to give it. Yet it is currently taboo to question and apply logic to mindsets and beliefs.

This disconnect is why many logical people and "empathetic" or "emotional" people fail to cooperate effectively. Our brains have evolved to do both, and evolution does EVERYTHING strategically. Finding harmony between logic, mindsets, emotions, and beliefs is often difficult but it is essential to elevating humans to the next stages in evolution.

Extremely "emotional" people often feel like logical people aren't in touch with their emotions, or don't feel emotions as deeply. Often "emotional" people place more value on the their current feelings and emotions than the future. In some cases, placing so much value on the present that it becomes illogical and detrimental to themselves and others. Many "emotional" people fail to grasp that feeling a strong emotion doesn't always merit an immediate actionable response. Often immediate actionable responses that aren't pre-planned with effective logic leads to creating a worse situation. Various feelings and emotions decrease the activity in the logical thinking portions of the brain.

I argue that logical thinking and logical action is the more effective route to pursue. A balance between logic and emotions is necessary. But emotions

---

[1] Being directly and unequivocally opposed

2

are substantially harder to quantify, and your logical thinking(or lack thereof) directly effects your emotions. Logical thoughts(theories, mindsets, beliefs) can be tested to see if they are subjective truths or objective truths. If your thoughts are logical they are closer to objective truths. The closer your reasoning is to the objective truth the more effective your results will be.

Objective truths are the rules by which our universe operates. Objective truths are true independent of your belief. The pursuit of sound logic, followed by application of sound logic is the most effective way to succeed in our universe. Accurate logic based on objective truths, is objectively the right course of action. There is rarely a sound argument to value emotions over logic, because emotions are an after effect of other variables. Accurate logic is always accurate. Accurate logical thought can be used to control, harness, enhance or reduce emotions. Your emotions directly correlate to your perception of reality and that perception is directly effected by how logical or illogical your current thoughts and mindsets are. Valuing logic more than emotions enough to make logical decisions before you act leads to better decisions for your current self and for your future self. Harmony between logic emotions is essential.

Once you start acting in ways that are lead by logic you can use your emotions in a way that best benefits yourself and others. Through practice and repetition, the increased use of logic and logical action will often lead to better harmony with your emotions. Since continued action compounds exponentially the extremely intelligent and logical people develop a level of emotional control that is hardly fathomable to people who aren't currently as logical or intelligent. Increasing your levels of intelligence and your ability to think logically can lead to better emotional control, but that doesn't necessarily mean you will feel emotion less. It is equally probably that you will feel a variety of emotions more deeply. All people perceive reality differently and feel emotions differently. Taking logical action guarantees that regardless of how you feel you will be taking action in a manner that is best for yourself or your goals. That may appear unemotional to people viewing it from a one dimensional viewpoint.

Being logical or emotional aren't two independent traits, or unchangeable ways of being. They are effected by how you consciously choose to think and act. Emotions will not change logic or the objective truth of the universe. Understating the objective truth and logic can change your emotions. The weak argument that some people are logical and others are emotional is flawed. All people are both to varying degrees. There are fairly obvious issues with letting emotions control your life and lead your decision making. "I'm emotional" has evolved into a very poor justification of inferior(objectively) decisions, actions, and behavior. The probability that you feel more deeply than all of your peers is low. To make an emotional response that is illogical, forces you to operate in a way that works against the laws of the universe. Which is why most people will realize at a later time that they made an illogical decision.

To test your current ability to think logically, there are some effective IQ test. There are also various emotional intelligence test. The current versions of both test have flaws yet some can give you an adequate assessment of your current ability. Another method that can test your logical processing ability without some of the flaws of the IQ test, is assessing your mathematical ability. Math has pre-established constant variables so you can achieve an objectively correct answer. How well you complete mathematical problems can show your current level of logical processing ability. Most IQ test have various mathematical questions because of math's innate ability to test objectively correct processing. You can use the IQ test to find out which areas could use the most improvement. Strengthening your logical processing ability will enable you to better process objectively, which helps you better understand the laws of the universe. Possessing a relatively high logical processing ability doesn't guarantee accurate thought, yet it helps formulate accurate conclusions. This is why many world views, philosophies, and religions lead to conflict, because so many people are opposed to assessing, and changing their mindset(s) to align with logic.

To change your mindset, assess yourself and think about what beliefs you hold that contradict the reality you are trying to create. Are your beliefs true and absolute? Where do your beliefs and mindsets come from? Do people that have similar mindsets to yours typically have the life that you desire? Does your mindset promote health, wealth, happiness, and prosperity? Do you enjoy living life with your current mindset? If the answer to any of these questions is NO, assess why you choose to keep these mindsets?

Pessimism and optimism are two mindsets. Optimist tend to live longer, and live happier more fulfilled lives than pessimist. The only difference is the mindset which they choose to live by.

It makes sense that the people who tend to view reality with a negative lens always find more negativity, because that is what they seek.

"We don't see things as they are, we see them as we are." ~Anaïs Nin

"Everybody in the world is seeking happiness—and there is one sure way to find it. That is by controlling your thoughts. Happiness doesn't depend on outward conditions. It depends on inner conditions. It isn't what you have or who you are or what you are doing that makes you happy or unhappy. It is what you think about it." ~Dale Carnegie, How to Win Friends and Influence People

Your current mindset is a choice and continuing to live by a mindset that isn't working for you is a poor choice. Some people adopt the mindset that you need to make mistakes to learn from them, while others adopt the mindset that it's easier to learn from other peoples mistakes to limit your own. Your mindset(s) affect how you think, how you learn, and how you live every part of your life.

Many survivors of slavery and the holocaust have overwhelmingly positive mindsets. Amidst some of the most vile atrocities that humans have endured, many survivors learned the key to happiness and inner peace by controlling their mindset(s) and their *focus*. The key is intentional directed *focus* on thoughts of happiness, love, positivity, gratitude, and putting effort into enjoying life and living it fully in the present moment. The correct mindset can benefit you in any situation. These people also have knowledge from one of life's most beautiful tools, perspective. Perspective gives you the opportunity to truly appreciate all of the moments of your life. Perspective can minimize your worst moments and maximize the quality of your best moments.

Many people never change their mindset and never evolve passed the thinking of their teachers. To grow you must evolve. If you want to grow you must be prepared to change. You can choose to keep the mindset you have or you can choose to develop new mindsets that will bring about a new reality. Study people that have the reality you wish to create and learn how they think, and what mindset(s) lead them to the success that you seek.

Adopt a mindset that *focuses* on accountability. The beauty of accountability is that it's always easier to change yourself than to change the world. It should be a great relief to find out that you are the cause of your problems. You are the author of your fate. Control what you can, and accept what you cannot, but highly value accountability so you can always strive to increase what you can control, therefore increasing your control over your reality.

We have access to nearly infinite information at our fingertips. You simply have to commit to using it. Adopt a mindset of growth and commit to learning. If you don't like your current situation find what you can do to change it. In the entirety of the universe you are the thing that you have the most control over.

Think about 3 things that are negatively affecting your life. Assess your mindset(s) towards these things. See what changes you can make to your mindset(s) that will change your circumstances.

2

Thinking

Thinking may sound normal but simply try to think of one thought that is actually yours. An opinion that is original, and unique that you can actually call your own. You may soon realize thinking is not a common as it should be.

In our current reality with access to nearly infinite information, it may seem impossible to discern the quality of information. One of the constantly increasing dangers of our information systems is bias. Companies have developed algorithms to find out what you think and give you more information to support your beliefs increasing conformation bias and driving wedges between differing views. With these systems people feel emboldened about their beliefs, and there is less understanding, tolerance, acceptance, and discussion.

This is an extremely dangerous phenomenon that can lead to many conflicts due to opposing world views. It removes people from reality and only shows people what they want to see, or information that triggers a response. With nearly unlimited information available, there is also much disinformation, and incomplete information circulating. People are becoming ideologically possessed, they stop thinking for themselves and just believe in concepts(if you don't understand the danger of this find a history book and study fascism). Information and misinformation are powerful and dangerous tools, that is why it is essential to live in truth and search for truth.

Our nearly limitless access to information has led to false awareness, a "woke" society. "Woke" individuals take small pieces of information usually incomplete or false and form ideas, theories, and opinions while neglecting the search for truth, validity, and accuracy. This phenomenon gives the appearance of intellect without the due diligence or accountability required in spreading information. Fake awareness is the blind leading the blind.

There is much danger in sharing information with others. Personal truths being illogical(objectively false) are dangerous but they are personal and you are currently free to think illogically. Yet when you choose to spread your illogical truths with other people the potential danger increases exponentially. Especially when the personal truths are accepted or believed to be objective truths. So there is a moral argument to be made that you have a responsibility to tell the truth. There should be a certain amount of responsibility and accountability when spreading information. The greater your influence and impact on others, the greater your moral responsibility should be. This is why truth is valued in most religions and philosophies and lying is legally punishable. To allow proven liars(intentionally or unintentionally) to influence you is dangerous. There is danger in tolerating objective falsehoods, even if they are subjective truths. This is why some people are imprisoned in mental institutions, their objectively false subjective truths make them extremely dangerous to themselves and to society.

The evolution of science and the increased learning of proven objective truths substantially alters societies. This is why many religions of the past have not survived. It is hard to convert people to a religion riddled with objective falsehoods. People, religions, and societies that accept objective truths and use that knowledge to work in harmony with the laws of the universe grow exponentially compared to people that don't. Institutions built with a foundation of objective falsehood usually crumble. Many religions and philosophies have contradictions. The point at which a contradiction arises is when you know there is a flaw somewhere in the logic. A contradiction is proof of non objectivity and imperfection. There are no contradictions in objective truths. This is one of the reasons why many intelligent and educated people denounce pre-established religions and turn to spirituality and/or science{Appendix 2}. They shift from accepting what they are told is the objective truth and begin thoroughly searching for the objective truths/the laws of the universe/God. This involves a level of difficulty and responsibility that many people don't want to undertake.

The most successful religions adapt their interpretation of the religious text(s) to align with the understood objective truths known at the time. Effective philosophies involve harmony between experience(individual and collective), logic, and fundamental principles(scripture). If the principles don't align with logic it will be hard to gain followers. When the principles don't align with experience then it isn't practical. When experience aligns with logic there can be understanding. When experience, principles, and logic are synchronized then there can be understanding and order.

People are often fairly agreeable to laws/rules that align or agree with objective truths, if they can understand the connection. Most people agree that these types of rules have an overall positive impact. This is not surprising since humans have evolved to think logically. Another reason religions struggle is because they state rules, ideas, and concepts without giving adequate explanations. So even if the religion/philosophy is stating objective truths, if their followers can't easily comprehend why it's the truth then it may not resonate with them and they will more easily oppose the rules. This is why the most effective parents and teachers understand the importance of comprehension. This is also why many societies repeat the same mistakes, the problems will continue to arise until you can adequately educate the youth about the fundamental principles required for success, and why the methods are effective.

Do not believe anything simply because you have heard it, read it, or even seen it. Don't blindly follow rules because they are the standard and they are commonly favored. Don't blindly follow your teachers, elders, peers, or priest. Don't blindly follow traditions simply because they have lasted for many generations. You should devote time towards thorough observation, research, experiments, and analysis.

Most people hold strong core beliefs and values that are referred to as sacred values. Sacred values are usually taught early in life, regarding morality, religion, justice, and views of right and wrong. Sacred values help the human brain follow the established dogma, and feel connected to their community. Many people will fight to the death to protect these sacred values and these values rarely change without a drastic shift in thinking or mindset(s).

The typical brain processes sacred values in a unique and alarming way. When sacred values are questioned or referenced the activity in dorsolateral prefrontal cortex(which is involved with self control, thoughtfulness, decision making and deliberation), decreases or shuts off. While the activity in the ventromedial prefrontal cortex(which is involved with emotions and social judgments) becomes active. Some studies have shown that the inferior frontal gryus(which is involved with rule retrieval) becomes active during this time as well. These effects are the results of our survival instincts and our brains trying to stop us from disconnecting from our base societal group, by dismissing logic, and reason for the sake being accepted to increasing survivability. This is a minimal example of power and the dangers of the brain. Knowledge of these processes can help you evolve past primitive instincts, and begin to think for yourself.

If you pick up a history book, you will quickly see the vile atrocities that were commonly accepted. You may quickly realize how few people desire to think for themselves, and go against the majority and the pre-established dogma.

Assess your sacred values. Are they logical, where do they originate, what reason where they created for, do you want to keep them, do they align with the life you want to live, are they just, fair, reasonable, and practical? If you are not willing to question your sacred values and core beliefs, you are simply a computer programmed to run someone else's code.

Most of your established routines, habits and the things you identify as were learned from your parents. Your parents learned from their parents and that cycle repeated for centuries. Your pre-programmed operating system may be thousands of years old, obsolete and simply based on survival. If you want be free to create yourself and achieve your goals you must first question your programming, then learn, unlearn, learn and adapt.

The most successful people do everything in there life strategically. Their sleep schedule, eating habits, learning techniques, their associates, and routines are all selected by themselves(consciously or unconsciously) to achieve whatever life goals they desire. The "self[2]" most people cling to has nothing to do with themselves, it is pre-established programming from your society and circumstances. Don't get stuck being "yourself"(the way your currently are). You must become fluid like water. No matter what container you put water in it will adapt, contort, or conform. With any glass you use, water will fit perfectly. In the cold it can harden and freeze. In heat it will boil steam or evaporate. Yet in every form water remains useful. Once you drop the fake, per-programmed "self" you can become fluid. You can adapt to any situation, evolve, and remain connected to your "true self".

To be free you must think and make your own decisions. Many people think this level of conscious decision making is too difficult or tedious. Yet if you don't determine every controllable aspect of your life, then someone else will or already has. Thinking is a requirement of freedom. You can't be free if you can't even determine what freedom is. Thinking is a requirement of living. Without thinking you may survive but you will not live.

How long will a good person remain good, while blindly following rules?

I urge anyone who wishes to think for themselves to listen to opposing arguments, viewpoints, and perspectives whenever they formulate an opinion. If your mind is not open to change, then you must count yourself as part of the problem. Always keep an open mind, because you don't know what you

---

[2] the combination of elements (such as body, emotions, thoughts, and sensations) that constitute the individuality and identity of a person

don't know, and what you do know is constantly changing.

"If you would be a real seeker after truth, it is necessary that at least once in your life you doubt, as far as possible, all things." ~Rene Descartes

You should value truth more than you value being correct. It's natural too misunderstand and to be wrong. The easier you can accept being wrong the easier it will be to learn, unlearn, relearn and adapt. To be open minded is to accept that your knowledge is limited and be willing change your way of thinking.

Original thought is creation, making something from nothing. It is something many have the power to do and few actually utilize. To some people it may seem difficult to generate ideas, but many have never been taught how. Many schools teach people to listen, repeat, regurgitate, and obey. Thinkers listen, process information, formulate opinions, and change their views with new information. Thinkers have the ability to change their inner reality and create a new outer reality.

There are countless ways to think, yet one of the greatest methods I have found for logical and scientific opinion forming and thinking is the scientific method. The scientific method involves observation, formulating questions, research, devising hypotheses, experimentation, analysis, reporting findings and conclusions.

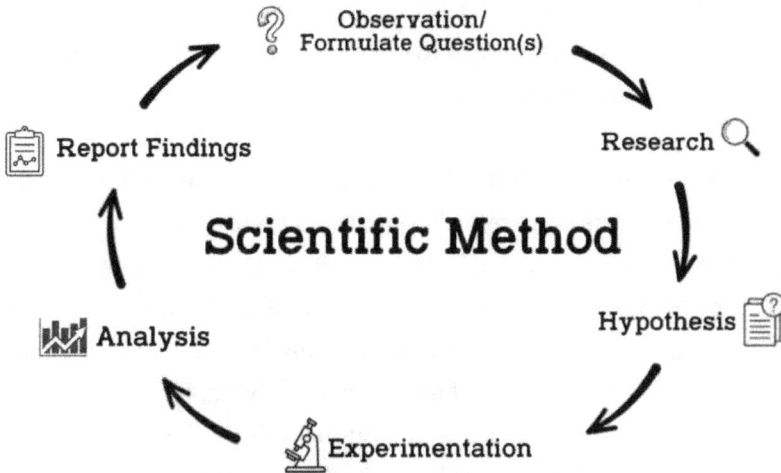

This method is so simple it is taught to children, and so powerful it is used by some of the greatest minds to ever walk this earth. It's a seemingly complete process that allows you to observe, learn, devise a theory, test the validity, assess data, and form new opinions based on scientific data. This method is a constant loop that always allows for learning and strengthening of the hypothesis. It allows for biases to be limited and/or removed to form better judgments and conclusions. This process is one of the great achievements of humanity, yet sadly it is under utilized. If you wish to achieve new success start applying this simple method to your life and solve problems. The more you use this process, the more you will become accustomed to solving problems easily and often, while using sound logic and reasoning.

This simple method allowed Leonardo DaVinci, Thomas Edison and Albert Einstein to invent, create, and change the course of humanity. The "greatest minds" and highest achievers in the world do simple things well, repeatedly. "geniuses" break down seemingly complex problems, into simple problems, and solve them. If you also wish to solve difficult problems follow the same method.

DaVinci simply observed everything, he studied nature, and humanity. He was always studying, learning, and questioning. Edison formulated theories and ran test until he could prove or disprove his theories.

The best way to solve problems is to discover the root cause of problem and fix it. Often times people try to remedy symptoms while ignoring the root cause. A common example is when people try to get society to stop using certain words, terms, or phrases. If the intent was to degrade or make someone feel bad, then the proposed solution does nothing to solve the real problem. Languages and vocabulary are constantly changing and evolving. Removing words from the language just leaves a void, and with most things when there is a void it will undoubtedly be filled. This is the perfect example of humans not truly understanding the root cause of their problems.

If you start examining the root cause of your problems, your life will becoming exponentially easier. Many people experience various symptoms of the same problems for a majority of their life and wonder why they are unhappy with their life. One of the principles behind evolution is adapt or go extinct. You can't adapt if you don't understand the root cause(s) of the problem.

Thought creates reality. Humans typical come up with ideas and use their bodies to carry out the building of our ideas. Yet many people think it's impossible to create items in the physical reality directly from thoughts. Yet generating an idea is the act of creating something from "nothing". If humans have the ability to create anything in the mind what is so different about creating in the physical realm. I theorize the power is within our capabilities, the real question is how.

What seems impossible, once accomplished quickly becomes the norm. The task of a visionary is to see a vision in their mind, and to alter reality to create that vision.

Many religions believe humans are made in the image of God. While some people interpret that as our physical form is similar to God. I ask why would an all powerful entity need a physical form. Maybe humans have the power to create just like the creator.

How is currently the issue. I believe that since the idea has been created its only a matter of time until outer realities reflect inner thoughts.

This may seem mystical to the logical mind but currently the culmination of logical thought has lead to two fields math and science. Math is fundamentally a system of numbers humans created to calculate and quantify the workings of the universe. Science is the attempt to study, theorize and try to logically understand our reality. Both systems were formed by humans to try and understand our shared reality. The current culmination of these fields is called quantum mechanics. My current understanding of quantum mechanics is that quantum mechanics has currently lead us to believe that at the smallest level of our physical reality(that we can measure) is fundamentally indeterminate(but not random) and it needs a conscious observer present to "exist" as we perceive it. Our physical reality is made up of the quantum realm. The quantum realm cannot exist without a conscious observer. Therefore our REALITY CANNOT EXIST WITHOUT A CONSCIOUS OBSERVER.

Mind is essential to matter, and matter is essential to the mind. So it seems mind and matter are codependent. Some Buddhist refer to this phenomena as dependent origination. I believe that the quantum realm being indeterminate means there is some type of order or system to our universe yet we can't currently predict the results. As I will discuss later in this book, we may not have a complete grasp of the system of our universe but we can tap into forces that will alter the results.

Everything we perceive as real(physical) is made up of things that we don't currently regard as real(physical).

Surprisingly as far as we understand, it appears the quantum realm doesn't behave by the same rules that our physical realm does, but our physical reality is made up by the quantum realm. If humans are conscious observers, and reality cannot exist without involvement from a conscious observer, then humans are fundamental to the existence of reality, and humans probably can alter that reality. The important question is why the quantum realm behaves differently than the physical realm. My theory is that consciousness is fundamental to reality and expanding our collective consciousness is the key to unlocking our full potential and expanding our ability of creation. I believe that dissolving self limiting beliefs is one key to expanding consciousness.

My current belief is that for conscious entities everything, even the workings of the universe is potentially understandable. If it doesn't appear that way, then you don't have all of the information, you aren't living in truth, or you don't wish to understand.

The premise behind logic is, given the same information you will come to the same conclusion. If we humans are indeed logical creatures, the main reasons we come to different conclusions are because we have different information, or we aren't thinking logically(bias).

I offer some practical tools to stimulate your thinking brain.

If you want to think, simply ask these simple questions constantly, WHY and HOW. These are the thinking questions. Children naturally ask them often. Curiosity is a natural byproduct of the mind. Thinking is natural in humans, if you don't think than it is probably because you have been taught not to think.

Write down ideas that pop into your head. When you have vivid dreams, or ideas that make you curious, write them down to later assess and explore them.

Many people don't realize that they love learning. Many people falsely equate school to learning, and let a few bad teachers ruin learning for them. Great thinkers throughout history fell in love with the process of learning which lead them to do and discover great things. Everything has a process or system and once you discover the process everything becomes easier. Successful leaders, entrepreneurs, athletes, actors, artist, doctors and scientist fall in love with the process of constantly learning.

Devote time to strengthening the brain. From a young age the parents of Nikola Tesla gave him daily exercises in memory, reasoning, and other mental activities. The brain is a muscle and muscles gain strength through use.

3

Mind

"It is not enough to have a good mind, the main thing is to use it well." ~Rene Descartes

The mind is the thing we have the most control over in the universe, yet I believe most humans still have very much to learn about their minds.

Feelings are simply thought detectors. Bad feelings are just your minds alarm system, telling you to reassess your thoughts and commit time to your mind.

A good feeling is your mind telling you that you are doing something correct, and it would like more of the stimuli that caused this feeling.

For most practical purposes the simplified equation for emotion(s) is:

PERCEIVED REALITY(experience) / EXPECTED REALITY(thoughts) = Emotion

$$ER / PR = E$$

*In the above equation "/" is not an adequate variable to adequately explain the correlation between PR relative to ER, and the weight of each variable changes relative to numerous factors. Yet this is a simplified equation for practical purposes and understanding. *

Your expectation compared to your perceived reality brings about an emotional response.

If your experienced reality exceeds your expectation you will be happy and feel positive emotions. If your experienced reality is worse than your expected reality you will feel negative emotions. Also if your expected reality and/or thoughts are overweeningly negative you will likely constantly feel negative emotions. If your thoughts are overwhelmingly negative even a good experienced reality can still lead to a negative emotional response.

If your experienced reality is more positive than your constant negative thoughts you may feel positive emotions, but with this way of operating the positive emotions rarely last.

Be wary of anyone who is in a constant state of emotional distress. That is a sign that they struggle with their view of reality(ER,PR) and that is a dangerous trait. The left side of the equation can be controlled by logic and reasoning and if a person struggles to stabilize that half of the equation then that person is potentially hazardous to themselves and others.

Now it is probably clear to you why optimist are usually happy, and pessimist are usually unhappy. In both cases the typical thoughts and mindsets tip the equation towards a specific direction.

I will let you think and choose which of the variables in the above equation you would like direct your energy towards changing.

Most people take the reactive approach and *focus* on dealing with negative emotions after they occur. Most people usually find various forms of escape to cope with their negative emotions, not realizing that changing the left side of the equation can actually cure their suffering and give them tremendous power. A proactive approach to this equation will lead you to the root cause of your problems and give you the power to limit or be free of suffering. The key to controlling your emotions is controlling, your perceptions, expectations, mindsets, and thoughts.

I urge you to remove all self limiting beliefs they are extremely detrimental to your mind and your potential. Humans are constantly evolving, and nearly all humans don't know what they are capable of, or what their limits are. To place limits on yourself is the ultimate enemy of progress. Our current reality is made up of countless seemingly impossible occurrences. Contemplate what the probability of your existence is. What are the chances of you being chosen to exist versus the other sperm, what are the chances of your parents meeting. Think for a second how many variables had to come into play for the big bang to create our universe. Simply existing as a conscious entity is improbable, so don't limit yourself to what seems possible or probable. If we don't know the limits of our abilities, it is essential that we believe in ourselves, that is the only way we can test our abilities.

Take the time to develop and strengthen your mind. It is a muscle that can be strengthened just like your physical body. The navy seals and the most elite warriors on the planet train and test the mind, because they know mental fortitude is the key to success in the most dangerous situations. One of the navy seals philosophies is to break soldiers down and rebuild them stronger, and repeat that process for continuous improvement. Sadly very few people take time to strengthen their mind. Take a second to recap your daily routine, and ask yourself how much time do you devote to your mind. Is the time you devote to your mind comparable to how much you value your mind?

To master your mind you must control the content you intake, especially for children and those weak of the mind. Weaker minds are easily molded in any direction, strive to obtain mastery of the mind.

The conscious mind is most commonly referred to as the mind. But the subconscious mind is a vital part of the mind. An attempt to control both is an attempt at mastery of the mind.

It is believed by many that most of the brain develops between birth and the age of six, when humans are less conscious. While the conscious mind may be mostly dormant the subconscious absorbs everything. Babies don't even comprehend impossible, they see and start experimenting with how. Babies don't question if they can walk, they try until they can walk.

Have you ever wondered why people who trust their "gut", "instincts", and intuition tend to be more successful. Have you ever wondered why mystical people tend to predict things, and understand things that don't make sense to the logical conscious mind. My theory is that they are more connected with their subconscious mind. Whether they understand it or not, the conscious mind may rest, sleep, or may be limited, but the subconscious mind is always paying attention, learning, studying, assessing, and evolving. When you sleep the subconscious mind is still at work. When you don't feel safe and don't consciously know why, your subconscious mind may be realizing something you don't.

When you meet people for the first time your subconscious mind formulates calculated opinions about them nearly instantaneously. That is why people say first impressions are important, because most communication is nonverbal. The subconscious mind can process information at a rate that is nearly impossible to comprehend. The subconscious mind can compute faster than any computer ever created. Lucky for us the conscious mind can effect the subconscious and vice/versa so mastery of the mind can truly lead to nearly unlimited potential.

Hyperthymesia is a rare condition that allows people to remember nearly every event in their life with great precision. My theory is that these people have a unique access to their subconscious mind, and as I have stated the subconscious mind is always paying attention to everything. There are some theories that biological, genetic, and psychological factors play into getting hyperthymesia. I do agree these factors play a big roll in brain formation and operation of the mind so this is not surprising.

I would like to make a disclaimer. Your subconscious mind can be negatively affected by your conscious mind. If you are constantly in a state of trauma or stress and if you hold negative or untrue beliefs your subconscious mind can deceive you. That is a reason why I believe your mindset and living in truth are essential to mastery of your mind.

If you want to connect with your subconscious mind a key tool is truth. Reality is subjective but you must live your truth. Always pursue truth. Living in truth is a key to inner peace. Many people think they live in truth but have no peace, how can that be. Pursue truth until everything makes sense.

I cannot definitely say I believe in universal truths, but I do know the value of truth.

Failure to live in truth and acknowledge reality for any reason can have severe consequences. This is why history constantly repeats itself because people will not dissolve their biases and accept truth. Yet I believe subconsciously we know truth and it resonates with us.

I believe that truth resonates with conscious entities to help understand their base nature and/or the nature of reality. This resonance with truth helps quench their natural curiosity. I believe that one form of enlightenment is becoming one with the truth and fully understanding it. I believe there are very few things if any that are absolute and universally true, but the things that are, are the key to enlightenment. People who fail to accept their truth doom themselves to a life full of self deception. It is nearly impossible to know true peace, when you don't trust yourself. When you choose to self deceive you are subconsciously aware of your deceit, which is why it is nearly impossible to know peace.

There are typically two types of liars in the world, people who lie to themselves and people who lie to others. In some ways the former is substantially worse. The man who lies to others must accept his own truth and then choose to deceive, the person who lies to himself is truly lost.

"This above all to thine own self be true." ~ William Shakespeare

If you start to understand the subconscious you understand the true power of knowledge. Our brains have a RAS(reticular activation system). The RAS helps filter the vast amounts of stimuli and information your brain intakes and makes it understandable to your conscious mind.

With the RAS once you learn something new your brain starts to see it show up often. So the more things you learn the more things your mind can recognize, process and understand. To the conscious mind that is amazing, but to the subconscious mind that is almost unfathomable.

The RAS filters out information you are not interested in, or conscious of, and searches for things you believe in, or are conscious of(your brain sees what it wants to see, and what it searches for). The RAS is proof that your mindsets directly affect your view of reality. The RAS can filter information from your conscious mind nearly removing it from your perceived reality. The RAS may be the cause of many biases, and close minded views of the reality. If you have a negative or pessimistic view of reality, your RAS will search out things that justify that mindset.

To combat the flaws of this system you must expand your perception of reality, through learning and experiences. You must also consciously choose your mindsets, as they will determine how your brain perceives reality.

In the process of understanding and mastering the mind the distinction between the conscious mind and subconscious mind may start to dissolve. I believe one of the goals of mastery of the mind is to have control over the mind(subconscious and conscious) and have access to the full power of the mind.

One form of "enlightenment" is dissolving of the self/ego[3]/mind which can lead to understanding the connection between individual consciousness and the collective consciousness. The connection between one and all.

There is a common misconception that there is a such thing a overthinking, I don't believe that to be true. I believe that there are negative thoughts, and mindsets, but the brain and mind has evolved to think. You can't overthink but you can allow negative thoughts to take over your mind.

To strengthen the mind you must push the known boundaries of your capabilities. You must increase your mental fortitude through practice and training, to overcome your preconceived limits.

"Men are not prisoners of fate, but only prisoners of their own minds." ~Franklin D. Roosevelt

---

[3] A division of the psyche that serves as the organized conscious mediator between the person and reality

Take this time to think of your self limiting beliefs and how you can work to dissolve them. One common self limiting belief that many humans place of themselves is only writing with one hand. Humans can easily write with both hands, it is just a matter of repetition. Yet most people learn from an early age to be dominant with one side of their body, cutting their potential in half, needlessly. Simply because that is the norm and nobody questions it. Think about the various ways you are holding yourself back, and take action to fix it.

Practically, I advise meditating often, seeking to learn and evolve, trying to push past your preconceived limits, and believing in yourself. When you are about to sleep make sure that your last thoughts before sleep are positive. Make your subconscious mind work for you while your sleep. You can put on learning materials while you sleep, or affirmations. When your subconscious constantly nags you, explore why and take action. To remove self limiting beliefs remove "I CAN'T" from your vocabulary, instead think "HOW CAN I". Remove all negative self talk from your life. It may be challenging when you first start but every-time you catch yourself thinking negatively take note and replace it with a positive thought. It may seem tiring or annoying but discomfort is a great motivator.

I believe the body and mind are more naturally inclined to positive thoughts, so through conscious reprogramming of your thoughts your subconscious will continually help you achieve your positive aims. To take control on your mind, start your day off *focusing* your mind. There are many ways to start your day depending on what your desire. Here are a few options, take a few minutes to meditate and bring your mind to the present, take some time to visualize the day you want to have, visualize your goals, plans, your purpose, and think of a few things that you're grateful for.

After you put effort towards controlling your mind, then speak affirmations to yourself. Keep a pen and notepad near your bed and right down your dreams, it may be your subconscious speaking to you. Always write down ideas as they come to you and act on good ones. Seek knowledge, try to read daily and your mind will be at work to constantly evolve. Push yourself out of your comfort zone daily, this will build mental toughness and test your "limits".

The placebo effect is yet another testament to the power of the mind. If you understand this effect, then you know the mind can heal the body simply by believing you can be healed. Please take a moment to truly ponder what that effect says about the power of the mind.

Next we study the body because the mind and body are connected, so maintenance of the body can strength or weaken the mind.

4

Body

Our brain and subconscious mind controls our neural networks which control or cells and all of the body functions, at a rate much faster than our conscious mind can comprehend. We know that our subconscious mind is in control of our body, and that our conscious thoughts and actions have an affect on our subconscious mind. So we must direct our conscious action towards control of the body.

Stress may start in the mind but manifest itself in the body in various forms. One of the most detrimental things to the human body is stress. It may be the deadliest disease that has ever effected humanity. A few ways stress manifest in the body are headaches, tremors, muscle spasms, sweating, colds, infections, herpes sores, rashes, hives, heartburn, stomach pain, nausea, constipation, diarrhea, and decreased or increased appetite. Continued stress disrupts the balance of your central nervous system, overworks the respiratory and cardio vascular systems. Stress can cause your heart to work too hard, and can weaken your immune system, so the body is less able to heal and protect itself. Stress alone can kill you, quickly or slowly through deterioration of the body. Stress also affects aging. Studies have shown stress can lead to shortened telomere length which accelerates the rate of biological aging.

Luckily most stress is created in the mind and can be controlled by mastery of the mind.

If you don't yet wish to attempt to master your mind, try a natural quick fix, laughter. Laughter is one of the oldest, easiest, and most effective ways to increase mood and heal the body and mind. *Focused* stress reduction and increased laughter increase your chances of surviving deadly diseases, and can reduce recovery time. Test have shown that forcing a smile on your face increases the amount of times you laugh. Try it, watch a comedy with a fake smile and see if you laugh more. I believe that if you laugh more your quality of life will surely increase.

Bad feelings, aches and pains are your bodies way of communication. Learn how to listen to your body. Understanding the chemical composition of the body aids in mastery of the body.

If you can harm and even kill yourself with negative thoughts, just imaging what healing, and creation you can also do with your mind. Our bodies are naturally self healing, we create, replenish and replace cells. On a cellular level we create constantly. (I still ponder why does reality seem to act differently on the microscopic, quantum and cellular levels)

Deoxyribonucleic acid (DNA) is the building block of the body. DNA passes down genetic information but it can also pass down other things. We know from countless studies that trauma can be passed down and we also know that many ailments of the mind can be passed down genetically.

In a study of mice that exposed mice to a cherry blossom scent and gave them electrical shocks on their feet. The animals learned to associate the scent with their fear of getting shocked. The offspring of the mice appear to have inherited the fear of the cherry blossom scent in their genetic code. Epigenetic mechanisms can dial the expression of particular genes. Trauma can literally affect the genetic code of animals and humans. Trauma oversimplified is a strong negative emotion combined with immense *focus*. DNA shows some examples of how the mind affects the body, your body and the bodies of your descendants. The key to overcoming DNA and other ailments of the body is *focus* and control of the mind.

I offer some practical solutions to improve your body. Spend time in the sunlight, spend time in nature, laugh often, find ways to exercise that you enjoy and exercise daily, eat healthy foods, meditate, and get adequate sleep. Also I propose routine dopamine detox's to counteract the over-stimulation common in our current society.

I will offer a practical method that you can use to harness your sexual energy and gain control over your mind and body. The method I will describe is for males and it ties together many of the principles of this book. I would like to state that I am not an expert in this practice, and I'm not aware of sufficient scientific data to prove this point. I currently believe in this practice and I think their currently is or soon will be scientific technology available to validate my points(or disprove them). Either way this is a theory you can test it out yourself(also various cultures have been experimenting with this practice for centuries).

Monks, priest, nuns, Taoist, Buddhist and various religions have been promoting abstinence, or controlled sexually interactions as way to reach higher spiritual levels. Some philosophies have rules against sex without giving an adequate explanation. Yet many of these philosophies tend to repel people because it doesn't seem logical. Sex is required to procreate, and our bodies have evolved to give us a strong innate desire to have sex. So to accept a doctrine that denounces sex, often leads to your mind fighting against the body. Humans perform optimally when things are in harmony not opposing. We humans usually have no desire to follow rules that make no logical sense, because our brains have evolved use and pursue logic.

There is a fairly simple solution. In some oriental philosophies they discovered a method that combines the perceived positive spiritual effects of abstaining from sex, but also quenches to biological desire to have sex. A solution that arguably produces more reward and substantially less risk. This process is semen retention. In this process, through devoted training and practice you can have orgasm(s) without ejaculating. Its known scientifically the male body uses sufficient energy to produce sperm. Every time you release sperm from you body, your body must work to replace it. And since this process is necessary for species survival your body values it highly and your body will dissipate vital energy to reaccumulate sperm quickly. This is a practical quick benefit of semen retention.

If you retain semen your body will have more energy, to be used for various purposes. In many oriental philosophies there are arguments that since sexual energy is needed for the continuation of the species it is one of the most natural and strongest forms of energy, and can be harnessed to elevate the body and spirit higher. Variations of this philosophy have appeared in numerous cultures throughout history all over the globe. Most of the cultures that value spiritual enlightenment mention a variation of this philosophy. Also many of the cultures that value spiritual enlightenment/advancement attest to the effectiveness of harnessing sexual energy through control of sexual urges.

In this process you can reduce the risk of pregnancy, gradual increase the pleasure of your orgasms, increase sex drive and increase the amount of time you can perform sexually. These are just some of the base level benefits of this practice. It is believed in many oriental philosophies that when you begin to master this practice you can start to harness your sexual energy and redirect it for various purposes.

There is also a variation of this process for women yet the benefits are more easily understood in the example of the males.

One fairly simple and fairly logical theory can easily change your perspective, and make seemingly illogical and impractical philosophies appear more practical, logical and desirable. If parts of this theory can be verified scientifically, then you get closer and closer to an objective truths. Objective truths are much more easily accepted, and as you accept them you continue to move closer and closer to understanding the laws of the universe.

5

Focus

"Anxiety is the dizziness of freedom." ~ Soren Kierkegaard

Focus is the tool used to counteract the aforementioned disease of the mind. *Focus* is a trade off, you get the power to accomplish something in exchange for a blindness of the wider world. The key to mastering *focus* is balance. Too much *focus* can lead to ruin, and too little *focus* will lead nowhere.

This is an oversimplification, but for practical purposes the conscious mind can only *focus* on one thing at a time. Often times we have numerous distractions which leads to split *focus*, which severely limits productivity. If you want to access the full potential of your mind, *focus* on only one task at a time with complete *focus*. Some studies say after every distraction it takes approximately 15 minutes to recenter your *focus* on a task. To counteract this phenomena remove distractions and train your mind to *focus* completely on one task at a time. More than half of all interruptions are self initiated. So try *focus*ing on strengthening the mind more than avoiding interruptions. A noisy mind is the biggest interruption.

"Perhaps the most difficult thing that a human being is called upon to face is long, concentrated thinking." ~Hugo Gernsbeck

In meditation you can quiet your mind with *focus*. The quieting of the mind and *focusing* on nothing is said to be one path the enlightenment. Transferring *focus* away from the "self" is said to be another path to enlightenment. A complete *focus* on healing can bring about healing. A complete *focus* on peace can bring peace. A complete *focus* on happiness can bring happiness. A complete *focus* on any task along with strong emotions and desire can exponentially increase your chances of achieve that feat.

Have you ever wonder why humans and animals that are in life or death situations can do seemingly impossible task. I theorize that when someone is in a life or death situation they have one singular *focus* along with strong emotions. Your subconscious mind, your conscious mind, and your body are all working together in peak synchronization to achieve a singular goal. That is *focus*.

If you can achieve this synchronization and *focus* in your life you will have the power to achieve seemingly impossible task. People commonly refer to this phenomena as being in "the zone". The zone is used by athletes, performers, artists, creators and many high performing individuals. The zone allows for peak performance, the body moves in complete synchronization with the mind, there is no hesitation or delay just *focused* directed action. Many of the worlds most elite soldiers say that directing all of their *focus* to one singular task is the key to precision, effectiveness, and extraordinary results.

If you wish to test your *focus* you can start with the mind. Try to quiet the mind by *focusing* on nothing. Try *focusing* on your body, by *focusing* on individual parts. Try to feel your pinky toes, your heartbeat, or your individual muscles and limbs. You may quickly realize your *focus* is rarely ever directed completely on one task, and you now have a few tools to fix that.

Many of the most successful people have a singular *focus* that they devote most of their time and attention to. If you are not where you want to be in life, assess your *focus*. Some have theorized that it takes approximately 10,000 hours of strategic work and effort towards any field for the average person to become a specialist. I believe that with deep *focused* work, along with the other tools mentioned in this book, you can reduce the required time and the ability to master skills becomes exponentially easier.

A practical tool to help strengthen *focus* is doing skilled work with your hands. My theory is that skilled work with the hands involves synchronization of the mind and body through directed action. Whether you believe my theory or not, this tool can help your sharpen your *focus*. This may also be why great artist can notice the smallest details that most people overlook.

With the power that the mind and emotions have on the body. *Focus* on the past and the future can have a drastic effect on your life. Often times people *focus* on the past and future and don't live in the present. The mind can feel and bring emotions from the past and future as if they are happening currently. In the mind there is no past, or future there is only the "present", and the present is where your *focus* lies. When you reminisce on positive memories you feel all the joy of the experience, and your body and mind are filled with positivity and happiness. When you are *focused* on negative memories your body and mind can feel stress similar to what you felt at the time of the memories. *Focus* on negative memories can lead to a variety of conditions, PTSD, depression, stress, and other diseases. The same principles apply to the future, thoughts of a positive future bring about hope, excitement, and joy as you feel the life you are about to live. While fear and dread of the future can lead to anxiety, paranoia, depression, eating disorders, and insomnia.

There is nothing in our mind that registers time. In our minds everything is happening now. This is why people often suffer more from imagination than from reality. So where you *focus* your mind is essential to mastery of your mind. *Focus* is the key to mastering the mind. To the noisy mind *focus* may seem difficult. An effective path to programming or reprogramming the brain is repetition. You must retrain your mind to unlearn negative habits and *focus* your attention on the positive. You can *focus* on positives memories, you can practice meditation and *focusing* on the present, and you can visualize the endless positive potentials of your future. But *focusing* on negatives can lead to anxiety and depression and these two illnesses are deadly because thoughts and emotions amplify and lead to more of the same thoughts and feelings. It is a deadly negative reinforcement loop.

Now that you understand the power of *focus* I will discuss the power of a life centered around a primary *focus*.

6

Purpose

"There is no defect except from within. There is really no insurmountable barrier save your own inherent weakness of purpose." ~Ralph Waldo Emerson

There are many purposes in life, and everyone must find their own. But having and knowing your purpose will propel you much further in life. Purpose gives you a directed *focus* and a reason(strong emotions or beliefs) and that is the recipe for success. Our brains are neurologically wired to pursue something. We usually obtain more pleasure from pursuit than from attainment.

"He who has a why to live for can bear almost any how." ~Friedrich Nietzsche

Purpose is *focus*, direction, clarity, and motivation. Many people are lost and don't seem to know their purpose. Many people let life happen to them.

"Life isn't about finding yourself. Life is about creating yourself." ~George Bernard Shaw

I believe that subconsciously we all know our purpose, but we must take action to create our reality. The more directed action you take the clearer the picture of your life will become.

Your primary purpose is your highest priority, it gives you a central *focus*,

33

and *focus* plus elevated emotions is the key to unlocking your full potential. When deciding your highest priority find the task or goal that will make nearly all other task easier or irrelevant. That is the simple rule to guide your search for a primary *focus*.

When you have a primary purpose you can direct nearly every action in your life towards attaining that purpose. If you are having trouble with decisions, determine which option will help you get closer to achieving your purpose. A purpose can add sufficient meaning to your life and will keep you centered towards the goal of your choosing. Most people don't mind hard and long work when it is directed towards a goal they truly desire to achieve. If your purpose fulfills you there are rarely any obstacles you will not overcome to pursue it.

With a purpose many activities that you previously avoided and disliked will be substantially more tolerable as you understand completion of these activities serves your primary purpose. With a purpose you will always have some motivation to succeed at your current task. With a purpose it will be easy to know when something doesn't belong in your life, if it adds no value to the attainment of your primary purpose consider removing it from your life and *focus* on something that does.

If you doubt the power of purpose research any person you deem successful and study their path to success, you will most likely see a primary purpose has guided their steps along the path to success.

If you don't currently know your purpose, that may be a sign that you don't know yourself. Take time to explore yourself, search for what drives you, what gives you motivation, and for what fulfills you. Your purpose can be as simple as making conscious effort to appreciate the beauty of life.

We all must find our own purpose. But I will offer a purpose here for anyone who is lost, and/or lacks the will to find their purpose at this time.

The purpose is, to improve yourself. It can be as simple as improving 1 percent everyday(quantifiable results are better for more objective thinking). With this purpose you must adopt a mindset of growth and change. You will always have a purpose because you can always improve. You will always be evolving and learning. You will fall in love with bettering yourself. 1

percent may seem small but continued it will lead to exponential growth, and achievement of nearly any goal. This purpose will make you strive to be the best version of yourself always, but only if you live in truth. This purpose is beautiful because it's a never ending cycle, with varying levels of difficulty, unlimited challenges, filled with curiosity, and endless chances at fulfillment. This is simply the beauty of life, the beauty of existing, it is the process of evolution, it is the process of creation.

Humans(individually and collectively) start progressing at exponential rates once they begin to develop effective mindsets and VOLUNTARILY seek and pursue challenges; and through these challenges EFFECTIVELY learn and EVOLVE, then use the acquired knowledge and changes to pursue their purpose. This process usually leads them to a better connection with themselves, and the laws of universe. Once you lock into this cycle(sustainable progression loop), inspiration, creativity and progress will seem to happen effortlessly. Once locked in this loop it will be easier to lock into "the zone". The mind a body will begin to synchronize, and you may begin to synchronize with the fundamental laws of the universe.

In hindsight please don't be fooled and believe that your current success is effortless, because every action you take during this process, compiles onto each other and truly leads to exponential growth and results. If you view your life as horrible and you feel that you are nowhere near where you desire to be this should be a great comfort to you; because if you understand how exponential growth compounds, then you know that your starting point is relatively insignificant. Please never underestimate the value of small changes in the correct direction.

No one is irredeemable, but the person who has the most power to help you, is yourself.

You hear similar quotes in nearly every religion or philosophy, but if you understand the above variables then you can understand that it's not just a pointless mantra, its a logical progression of evolution. If you agree that this is one of most effective methods of progressing, then you must note that the path to progress involves challenges. Challenges involve a certain level of discomfort. Initially the discomfort often seems substantially worse. So the most effective path to progress in not comfortable, and you must develop the habit of VOLUNTARILY choosing to be uncomfortable(at varying degrees) to achieve continued progress. People who understand this model of progress can and often do achieve success in many parts of their life.

Living with a purpose isn't just about achieving a specific goal, or arriving at a certain destination. It is about continually making progress, evolving, and striving to be a better version of yourself. The beauty is in the aspiration, the process and the journey.

People who retire and don't have a purpose die much earlier than retirees with a purpose, hobbies, and something to work towards. Freedom without purpose often fails to bring happiness. Religion is an effective tool partly because it gives people a purpose that they can always work towards.

To live with this purpose you must push yourself out of your comfort zone everyday, learn constantly, learn to love your current self while creating your new self. Constantly test your power of creation as you create your new reality. I encourage everyone to adopt this purpose, it is a mindset that may lead to much progress. This purpose is commonly referred to as a growth mindset.

It's normal to change your primary purpose as life progresses and your views change, but it is essential to have a purpose to make sure you are always in control of the direction of your life. So that you are living life and that life isn't happening to you.

If you now understand the power of purpose you may realize why an extremely comfortable life, free of challenges rarely leads to fulfillment, a belief of self worth and prolonged sustainable happiness. Often people who work hard and obtain an overly comfortable lifestyle, realize that they were more fulfilled pursuing the lifestyle than achieving it. Our brains reward system is designed to reward us when we are progressing. This is why the wealthiest and most successful people in the world work for nearly their entire life. This is also one of the reasons why societal models that try to achieve an overly comfortable utopia world often lead to great turmoil. Humans are designed to progress.

I offer a practical tip to help you derive a purpose. Write a movie about a possible life. In this movie make the main character everything you like, everything you think is morally good, and everything that fulfills you. Make the main characters life as amazing as you can fathom. Once you write a movie and dream up the world, find the one action or course of action that will most increase your chances of having a life similar to the movie, then start planning and take action.

In the next section I will discuss a concept and tool that can help in accomplishing nearly any purpose you desire.

7

Wealth

In many societies wealth is a tool to live life free, free to chase your dreams, freedom to spend your time doing what you want, freedom to explore your curiosities, freedom to pursue your purpose.

The steps to build wealth are very simple.

Live below your means.

This is done by saving more than you spend. Avoid debt, unless strategically. If you don't believe you can do this re-evaluate what you need. Many "needs" of current society are actually luxuries. Humans have survived with much less. If you feel you deserve nice things earn them. Don't buy things with money you don't have. This may have become common practice but it is not acceptable. Debt makes you a slave. Don't give away your freedom so easily. You must master this skill to be able to build wealth. If your expenses are greater than your income you will always operate at a deficit. For many people their expenses grow proportional to their income, so making more money isn't guaranteed to solve the issue. Proper money management is the key to financial freedom.

Add value to society and get paid adequately for the added value.

Money is the embodiment of the principal that people who want to deal, must trade value for value. Money is simply a value token. If you add more value then you should be paid more value tokens. If you want to make more money, then add more value to the world. This may seem hard, but the world is always changing and one simple way to add value to the world is to find a problem and create a solution. If there are problems in the world then there are opportunities. Problems will always evolve so opportunities for wealth will always be present. Think about what you don't like. Listen to what people often complain about. Contemplate what can make your life easier. Once you deduce these things, work towards devising solutions. People often have million dollar ideas, that they either minimize because they don't realize the value, or don't take adequate action towards transforming their ideas into reality. Start writing down your ideas, then take directed *focused* action towards making your ideas into reality. If you are adding value to society and not getting paid proportional to the value added; remove yourself from the situation, and find or create a system that ensures you get rewarded adequately for your added value.

Make your money work for you.

This is the process of generating passive income. Passive income separates your time from your money. Your time is limited, so you need to make money while preserving your time, that is one component of wealth. To do this you must learn how money systems work so you can make your money multiply. Many of the best money systems have been around for centuries, you just have to learn them. An easy way to better understand money systems is to learn HOW the business owner(s) is making money and building wealth from the system.

McDonald's is currently one of the largest corporations in the world. It has been reported that Ray Kroc the founder of McDonald's once asked some students what business he was in. They believed like most people that the primary purpose of his business is to make money selling hamburgers. He then educated them and told them that his primary business is real estate. He has made millions of dollars and created one of the most successful businesses in history selling hamburgers, but he understands the real value is in the real estate. Most of the McDonald's buildings are located in extremely valuable locations. Real Estate has historically been one of the most profitable and reliable businesses in the history of humanity.

So McDonald's as a company can loose their "primary" revenue stream, and still receive passive income indefinitely. This example perfectly illustrates that if you want to build wealth you must understand how money systems work, and what the best wealth creation systems are. The best systems are usually quite simple, and have been around for generations in various forms.

Another example of understanding businesses is casinos. Most casinos and gambling business models are to create a series of games in which the odds are systematically designed to be in favor of the business. Then casinos convince and/or deceive people into believing that the odds are in their favor by advertising the small percentage of winners. The customers have to lose for the business model to be effective, so its illogical to partake in a system designed for you to lose.

Someone who learns and lives by these steps should be able to go anywhere in the world and build wealth with this knowledge.

There are plenty of strategies to build wealth. This strategy is simple and has been used for centuries in various wealthy societies.

This mindset of building wealth is simple, easy to teach, and your wealth is directly proportional to your impact on society. You increase in wealth as you help others. If you impact millions you can make millions. This mindset builds wealth and attracts prosperity and abundance to all who live by it. Many people have negative mindsets of the wealthy and rich and that is a reason they rarely obtain wealth. You must have a positive wards wealth if you wish to attract it. With this mindset you understand that wealth and abundance are unlimited, you don't have to steal, or destroy others to build wealth and prosperity. Simply give more value to the world and get paid adequately.

The key to living in a wealthy and abundant society is to share this mindset and these simple steps. Simply giving someone money is just a band-aid and it doesn't solve the problem. The vast majority of lottery winners lose their fortune and return back to poverty, simply because they never learned how to manage money and earn wealth. This is one of the best gifts you can give future generations. If you teach people how to obtain wealth you will not have to give them money, but if you do they will know how to multiply it. This is often why many first generation rich people fail to build generational wealth, they fail to teach their children and spouses how to build wealth. For an organization to last the process(es) must be duplicable.

A way to measure your wealth is to calculate how long you can survive, while living the same lifestyle if you stopped working.

Now that I have showed you a simple and logical formula to wealth creation, I shall describe a method that can be used to bring wealth and anything else into your life.

8

Manifestation

"Our life always expresses the result of our dominant thoughts."~Soren Kierkegaard

Manifestation is the power of creation that is brought about by connecting the mind to the ether[4]/collective consciousness/power of universe. If there are rules that govern or limit our creation ability, can anyone know? I assuredly don't. I do know that the law of attraction is fundamental to this process of manifestation. The law of attraction simply states that what you put out will come back to you.

This law can refer to almost anything from thoughts, actions, energy, and frequencies. Due to the law of attraction if you wish to bring something into your life, then you can't take actions that work against your goal. You must be on the same frequency as the thing you wish to attract. Anyone who remotely understands the power of manifestation, and the law of attraction truly understand the importance of mastery of the mind, and controlling your thoughts.

Visualization is a great tool used to train the mind and body as well as manifest a new reality. Visualization is powerful because it *focuses* the mind. Practiced visualization has been shown to help with creativity, sports, learning,

---

[4]   A medium that permeates all regions of space and transmits transverse waves

testing, and skill development. When you visualize your neural networks are firing identical to the actual task you are visualizing.

Studies in neural plasticity have shown that the brain and nervous system are malleable and repetition combined with firing neurons in certain pathways can rewire the brain. Repetition is the essential tool to rewiring the brain and visualization is as easy method to alter the brain to develop new skills, habits, and abilities.

In the mind there isn't real or fake, there is only *focus*. You can visualize and develop skills and train your body without having to move your physical body. Visualization has been used to learn how to play the piano and to realign a broken spines. The possibilities are limitless.

The key to manifestation is to visualize, feel strong emotions, and have complete *focus*. You must have a clear and vivid picture in your mind of what you want to manifest. You must see, feel and live in the new reality, go over every detail in your mind's eye[5] and connect with that new reality. In the mind there is no sense of time. Your mind cannot tell the difference between reality, dreams, past, future, and the present, so you must feel and live your new reality to create it. Use all of your senses, visualize, smell, touch, hear, and taste your new reality. You should completely immerse yourself in the new reality. Once you create and hold the reality in your mind a portion of the creation process is complete.

Once you have a clear picture in your minds eye you must use the power of your emotions. Summon all of the emotions you will feel when you have achieved this new reality, feel why you want to live in this new reality, feel the emotions of your new self in your new reality. These strong directed emotions will summon the power of intent. Once you summon these strong emotions use the power of belief. Believe that this new reality is yours. Use your strong intentional belief to remove all self limiting beliefs, and to affirm to yourself that you are connected to this new reality. Believe in yourself and your power of creation. Believe in the power of the ether/God/the universe

---

[5] the site of visual recollection or imagination.

and trust that you are now connected to this new reality. The next step in the manifestation process is to receive. You must be ready and willing to receive what the universe/ether/God has in store for you. Be ready to seize opportunities as they will quickly begin to appear. Be ready to take directed action towards the manifestation of your goal. You must keep your frequency connected to the reality you wish to create, through positive directed action, through strong unwavering belief, through positive thoughts and through the law of attraction.

A beautiful tool to complete or speed up the manifestation process is gratitude. Gratitude is the final step in the manifestation process, because that is the emotion you feel when you receive something that you desire. Gratitude is one of the strongest positive emotions. So after you visualize and feel your new reality, conclude with the emotion of gratitude to supercharge your power of manifestation. If you struggle with having gratitude from something not in your current reality then practice gratitude for the things that you do have. In order to bring more things into your life that you are grateful for, you must first be grateful for the things that you have. This tool is so simple yet it will change your life, and your mindset. This is the process of creation.

This is just one method of manifestation. There are various versions of this process, but the principals are the same, you simply create a reality in your mind, you believe that it is yours and then you attract your new reality. Nearly every human who has succeed at a task knows some form of this process. I hope that you will begin to study this process and test the boundaries of human creation.

"Until you make the unconscious conscious, it will direct your life and you will call it fate." ~Carl Jung.

Another practical tool to help with your manifestation process is a vision board. Simply make a board with pictures of the reality you wish to create. You can add things you wish to manifest, pictures of yourself feeling the emotions you plan to feel in your new reality, pictures of the company you will have around you, any pictures that will bring you joy and keep the new reality fresh in your mind. Then place your vision board somewhere you can see it often. Familiarize your subconscious mind with this new reality. Look at your vision board daily and know that you are connected to that reality. You can place the vision board right above your bed so its the first and last thing you see at night, so that you can always realign your *focus*.

Setting a date on your manifestations is a tool that may be helpful. Adding a date to your manifestation adds decisiveness and intentionality which can strengthen your power of creation. The potential downside of adding a date to your manifestation is that you may achieve precisely what you ask for. If you try to manifest something in 10 years you may receive it in 10 years when you could have received it sooner. Adding specific details can better align your *focus* to the reality you are asking for. Make sure you're asking for exactly what you desire.

Too manifest a reality you desire you must *focus* on that reality. Many people put all of their *focus* on things they don't want and then wonder why it keeps happening. You must have complete *focus* on what it is you desire. The mind doesn't understand negatives. If I tell you "don't think about a bear", it becomes nearly impossible for you to not think about a bear.

The mind understands *focus*. That's why certain affirmations are negative.

"I will not be poor forever"
   "I will not fail"
   "I am not a failure"
   "I am not depressed"
   "I am not like my parents"
   "I am not fat"
   "I am not ugly"
   "I am not afraid"

Remove "not" from the above statements and you will clearly see where the *focus* lies. An affirmation *focused* on what you don't want isn't an affirmation at all, its a hex.

"What you resist persist." ~Carl Jung.

You can change the above affirmations and make them positive by shifting the *focus* to what you do want to manifest.

"I will be wealthy"
   "I will succeed"
   "I am successful"
   "I am happy and at peace"
   "I am the person I strive to be "
   "I am fit and healthy"
   "I am beautiful"
   "I am courageous"

or

"I can be wealthy"
   "I can succeed"
   "I can be successful"
   "I can be happy and at peace"
   "I can be the person I strive to be "
   "I can be fit and healthy"
   "I can be beautiful"
   "I can be courageous"

"If you hold an anti-war rally, I shall not attend. But if you hold a pro-peace rally invite me." ~Mother Teresa

If you still doubt the power of manifestation, I will provide a quote from arguably the greatest scientist and creator in human history.

"My method is different. I do not rush into actual work. When I get an idea I start at once building it up in my imagination. I change the construction, make improvements and operate the device in my mind. It is absolutely immaterial to me whether I run my turbine in thought or test it in my shop. I even note if it is out of balance. There is no difference whatever, the results are the same. In this way I am able to rapidly develop and perfect a conception without touching anything. When I have gone so far as to embody in the invention every possible improvement I can think of and see no fault anywhere, I put into concrete form this final product of my brain. Invariably my device works as I conceived that it should, and the experiment comes out exactly as I planned it. In twenty years there has not been a single exception. Why should it be otherwise? Engineering, electrical and mechanical, is positive in results. There is scarcely a subject that cannot be mathematically treated and the effects calculated or the results determined beforehand from the available theoretical and practical data. The carrying out into practice of a crude idea as is being generally done is, I hold, nothing but a waste of energy, money and time." ~Nikola Tesla

Nikola Tesla's creative ability was so amazing among his death in 1943 the U.S. governments Office of Alien Property confiscated most of his items and research. The FBI didn't declassify most of his research until 2016. Some believe many of his files are still missing. It is believed that of the 80 trunks originally confiscated only 60 were returned to the rightful heir.

If you still don't believe in the power of manifestation I offer a practical solution. You must still visualize the reality you wish to create. Visualize every detail of your reality. Visualize how you will live, what you will do and who will be with you in this new reality. This will get your subconscious mind *focused* on your new reality, so when opportunities present themselves you will be able to act and seize opportunities to create that reality. Keep your subconscious mind *focused* and working for you. Now take note of your new reality and work backwards. Make this your priority, and formulate a plan to achieve your goals. Most people have dreams, but not goals. Goals require planning and actionable steps to achieve them. Once you devise your plan, write down the steps and say them to yourself twice daily, when you awake and before you sleep(to program your subconscious). It is essential to make the steps actionable. To do this take your plans from years, to months, to days, and break them apart into habits. Habits are the key to a successful life. Develop the habits you need to create the reality you desire. This is the simple practical way to bend reality to your will, through organized directed action.

Once you develop your plan setup times to reassess your progress and keep yourself on track. It can be weekly, monthly, or yearly depending on your current level of discipline, but this step will keep you *focused* and in control of your reality. This step will give you a chance to appreciate your development and asses your successes and failures. If you aren't seeing the results your desire take accountability and reassess your habits and plans, adapt and evolve. Your outward reality is a reflection of your inner thoughts.

This level of planning will help you optimize your schedule and make sure nearly all actions you take are directed towards the creation of your desired reality. Habits dictate results, its simple yet most people fail to realize it. When motivation fails we regress back to our pre-established habits. If you doubt the power of habit then test this theory. You can simply go to any grocery store and look at peoples carts and their weight. Despite all the excuses you may hear, 95% of the time the outcome is a direct result of the habits. The most powerful companies and governments in the world spend billions on tracking data analytics, because they understand humans are predictable and small habits and actions lay out the blueprint of future.

Often times the magnitude of your goals is directly proportional to how you view yourself. So set goals worthy of the version of you that you want to create. Don't just set easy attainable goals, strive to achieve your wildest dreams.

In quantum mechanics one of the leading theories is the many-worlds theory. An interesting quantum phenomena is called quantum entanglement. I wont go into detail on these two subjects because there is plenty of literature about them. But one way to look at manifesting is to understand that there are all possible realities in the many-worlds theory or the metaverse and with your minds eye/third eye[6] you have to connect with the reality you desire and attach yourself to that reality through quantum entanglement. Quantum entanglement occurs faster than the speed of light and outside the realm of Newtonian physics and the physical reality, it is practically instantaneous.

"Any sufficiently advanced technology is indistinguishable from magic." ~Arthur C. Clarke

A simple example I can use to describe the law of attraction is a radio. There are many stations playing of many different frequencies, but you can't hear them unless you tune your radio to the same frequency as the station you want to hear. The frequency is always there you must have a device that can connect with it and then you must match frequencies. The principle is the same for attracting what you desire, you use your minds eye/3rd eye and tune into the reality you desire. We are beings made up of energy, and energy can never be created or destroyed only transferred.

"If you want to find the secrets of the universe, think in terms of energy, frequency and vibration." ~Nikola Tesla

I can't say I fully understand the power of creation, or the system(s) that control our universe but I do believe the law of attraction is a fundamental law of the universe. Some people refer to this phenomena as karma. Most people understand karma when it comes to actions but I also refers to thoughts.

Have you ever wondered why when you start your day and you stub your toe on the side of your bed, everything seems to go downhill from there. Continuous negative occurrences seems to happen to you. When you start your day off with a negative thoughts, you attract more of the same. When you start your day off with great news, the rest of your day seems to be filled with

---

[6] A point on the forehead relating to one of the chakras that is associated with enlightenment and/or mystical insight. Also referred to as the pineal gland.

positivity. This is not a coincidence this is the law of attraction. When you first awake the vail between your conscious mind and subconscious mind is thin, that coupled with strong emotions(negative or positive), has the power to attract large amounts of the same energy.

If you ever want a quick way to change your frequency then change your *focus*. To do this you can stop for a moment, take a few deep breathes, clear your mind and consciously redirect your *focus* on something positive.

Belief is *focus* plus strong emotions. History has shown us that a collective belief is something can bring about great progress. Religions are founded on the power of belief. Yet sadly many religions harness the power of belief while also teaching and instilling numerous self limiting beliefs. Often times religions, governments and leaders, channel the power of your belief to achieve their aims. Belief is using the power of the mind to alter reality. So use the power of belief to believe in yourself and create your reality. Take a moment and contemplate what prayer is. In most religions prayer is usually a variation of confession(living in truth), giving thanks(gratitude), asking for what you desire(request), praise(strong beliefs and gratitude), and quieting of the mind from outside noise(meditation and *focus*). This sounds quite similar to what I have stated. Clearly some have known the power of manifestation for ages.

"Therefore I say unto you, What things soever ye desire, when ye pray, believe that ye receive them, and ye shall have them."
~ Mark 11:24 KJV BIBLE

"And I say unto you, Ask, and it shall be given you; seek, and ye shall find; knock, and it shall be opened unto you. For every one that asketh receiveth; and he that seeketh findeth; and to him that knocketh it shall be opened."
~Luke 11:9-10. KJV BIBLE

"And Jesus said unto them, Because of your unbelief: for verily I say unto you, If ye have faith as a grain of mustard seed, ye shall say unto this mountain,

Remove hence to yonder place; and it shall remove; and nothing shall be impossible unto you." ~Matthew 17:20 KJV BIBLE

Prophets always have dreams or visions of the future that they believe in totally and fully, and accordingly reality bends to their will.

Martin Luther King Jr. had a dream:
   "That the sons of former slaves and the sons of former slave-owners will be able to sit down together at the table of brotherhood."
   "That my four little children will one day live in a nation where they will not be judged by the color of their skin but by the content of their character."
   "One day right there in Alabama little black boys and black girls will be able to join hands with little white boys and white girls as sisters and brothers."
   "With this faith, we will be able to transform the jangling discords of our nation into a beautiful symphony of brotherhood."

Nelson Mandela lived through apartheid but had a vision of a free Africa. He was sentenced to life in prison for freedom fighting. He used the time in prison too mellow(quiet the mind), to gain clarity(*focus*), to deepen his convictions(intent and strong emotions), and to read and learn(search for truth). From prison he became the face of freedom and one of the most powerful people in Africa. After 27 years in prison he was released. He ended apartheid in South Africa and helped bring in some peace and free elections. He was then elected the president of South Africa. He stated "Hope was always there and this is what saved us".

Roger Bannister was the first documented person to run a mile in under four minutes on May 6, 1954. Before this accomplishment many people didn't believe it was possible for anyone to run that fast. Humans have been running for eons, and this feat was truly amazing. Only 46 days later another amazing thing happened, John Landy completed the same feat. Countless people have done it since. This is a testament to the power of belief. Once people know something is possible, it happens more easily and often. Most limits that humans have they place on themselves. This phenomena occurs in every sport, every field, every science, and every way of life.

When humans first decided to place a person on the moon, it seemed impossible. There was no detailed plan, and it was completely uncharted territory. Many people believed it would never happen, yet the people who believed altered the course of human history. Scientist and engineers had to invent, create, and develop new technologies. All they had was a belief it was possible and access to the power of the mind. In a short period they invented technology at a rate never before seen in the history of humankind. A simple thought, followed by belief, followed by a *focused* determination to bend reality towards their goal altered the course of humanity.

As we now know the power of thoughts, we must also know the power of our words. It is essential to always mean what you say. To always mean what you say you must first live in truth. There is much power in words especially when spoken about oneself. When speaking about yourself it is often a self fulfilling prophecy so choose your words wisely and carefully.

Affirmations are verbal tools to manifest your reality. I recommend keeping your affirmations simple. You can start your affirmations with

"I can" or "I am". When you say affirmations, say them confidently, and believe it as you say it.

I recommend saying affirmations in the present tense, as if you already have what you are affirming. If you speak in the present tense you are resonating with the reality you wish to create.

Make sure your affirmations are concise and direct. If your affirmations are ambiguous you are more likely to attract a reality that you don't want. If your affirmations are vague you may get precisely what you ask for, but not what you desire. Use the power of intent and be clear on what you want to manifest.

I recommend not limiting your affirmations. If you wish to manifest $1,000,000 by June 23, 3035. I would recommend an affirmation stating "I will have AT LEAST $1,000,000 by June 23, 3035 or SOONER".

I recommend avoiding vague affirmations like "I am special"(what does that even mean). Get specific.

It is not a coincidence that the most successful people know exactly what they want, and believe it is theirs before they receive it.

Repetition is how you rewire the brain. Say affirmations continually until you believe them completely.

Affirmations are a powerful tool that allow you to use your conscious mind to directly speak to your subconscious mind. You can use this tool to create new versions of yourself and to create new realities for yourself.

Practically here are a few tips.

Never talk bad about yourself, not even while joking your subconscious mind is always on. Inside of almost every joke there is some truth. Negative self talk is the worse kind of self fulfilling prophecy. Making this one step can alter the course of your existence. Positive affirmations are a great tools to rewire your mind.

The path the great things are started with the smallest of steps. If you don't believe in the power of words try the plant test. Find two healthy plants, and put them in similar environments. For one plant speak only positive affirmations, for the other plant speak only negative affirmations. At the end of 30 days you should visibly be able to see the difference in the two plants and you shall see the power of words.

If you wish to try manifestation you can start with something small. It isn't easier to manifest something small, but it is generally easier to believe in something small, and belief is essential to success in manifestation.

"A person is the product of their dreams. So make sure to dream great dreams. And then try to live your dream." ~Maya Angelou

Most people have tapped into the power of creation, in some form, yet few if any fully understand what they are tapping into. How can you definitely know, when reality starts to bend to your thoughts. This may still seem abstract to some but anytime you increase your knowledge, intelligence, or power you increase your ability to bend reality to your will. Whether you choose the use this power, or not, it exist and simply understanding a fragment of it alters your perception of reality. With this power it may become hard to separate reality from a dream, but a byproduct of the power of creation is dissolving the vail of reality.

Your biases limit your reality. The easiest way to describe a conscious entity is

"I think therefore I am." ~ Rene Descartes

9

Psychedelics

You should accept the possibility that there is a limitless range of awareness that we don't currently have words to describe.
Awareness can expand beyond the your ego, beyond your identity, beyond everything you believe, beyond the limits of space and time, and beyond the differences which separate humanity.

Many people have described psychedelics as the tools of consciousness. Classic psychedelics is a term used to refer to a family of chemically similar drugs called tryptamines, this includes psilocybin(the active ingredient in magic mushrooms), dimethyltryptamine(DMT), lysergic acid diethylamide(LSD), and mescaline(the psychoactive component of peyote). These classic psychedelics have similar chemical structures to serotonin. Serotonin is involved with mood regulation, memory, and various other bodily functions. Most of your bodies serotonin is stored in the gut("trust your gut").

Serotonin	Psilocybin	Psilocin	LSD	DMT	5-MeO-DMT
$C_{10}H_{12}N_2O$	$C_{12}H_{17}N_2O_4P$	$C_{12}H_{16}N_2O$	$C_{20}H_{25}N_3O$	$C_{12}H_{16}N_2$ (Base)	$C_{13}H_{18}N_2O$

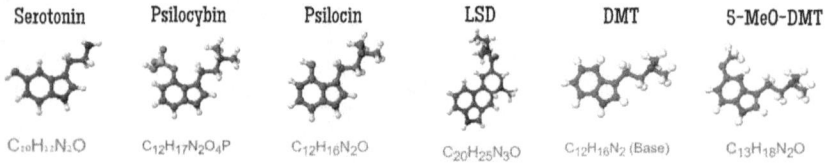

The classical psychedelics can all be eaten. They enter the bloodstream and bind to certain serotonin receptors in the brain and can alter your perception of reality for a period of time.

There have been various clinical test on psychedelics being used to treat a variety of mental illnesses and to help counteract substance abuse and addiction. Psilocybin test have lead to some of the most effective smoking cessation treatments every studied. In many studies a singular dose of psilocybin drastically helped reduce symptoms of anxiety and depression. A singular dose of psychedelic compounds can have lasting effects for the rest of your life. Some LSD studies have shown greater results at curing and reducing mental illness than nearly any other other drugs currently available. Studies of LSD and DMT on patients with a variety of mental disorder have shown long term lasting positive effects years after the initial single use studies.

In the late 1960's a growing psychedelic movement became a threat to certain political interest. Groups of younger people started using large doses of psychedelics with improper or no guidance. The mass media quickly demonized psychedelics and the United States government ran by Richard Nixon placed psychedelics and marijuana as schedule 1(the most dangerous legal category) substances. Schedule 1 substances are categorized as having a high potential for abuse and no currently accepted medical use in treatment. The later of those statements should certainly be reevaluated. 184 United Nations member states quickly followed suit and banned certain psychedelics. Promising LSD test funding dried up, and regulatory approval became nearly impossible. Yet most of the clinical research to date on psychedelics is still overwhelmingly positive.

The Nixon administration then created the DEA to enforce drug laws and to start infamous WAR ON DRUGS. Stanley F. Yolles the former director of the National Institute of Mental Health in 1970, resigned after publicly clashing with the Nixon administration. He was outspoken and known for saying that the penalties for illicit drug use were far more harmful than the drugs themselves. He accused the White House of cutting funds for federal drug abuse and alcohol control programs and applying political considerations in the appointment of candidates in scientific positions.

If his claims are true, this may paint a picture as to why these drugs are still illegal, and why some of the most promising drugs for a variety of mental illnesses and disorders don't have adequate scientific studies.

Psilocybe mushrooms are common on nearly every continent. Archaeologist suggest that psychedelic themed illustrations date back to 10,000 B.C.E.. The historically advanced Aztec society ate "mushrooms with honey".

The Spanish saw this practice as a threat to Christianity and brutally suppressed the "mushroom cult".

Steve Jobs the pioneer of apple, once stated that experiencing LSD was "one of the most important things in my life.". That is a powerful quote from a man whose inventions and ideas revolutionized modern technology, and altered the course of humanity.

Ancient societies made sure to *focus* on setting, mindset, and intentionality when using psychedelics. *Focus* is essential with psychedelic drugs, that's why the ancients societies used shamans and elders to guide people on their journey.

During psychedelic trips, regions of the brain that don't usually interact begin to communicate. There are some theories that say during this process there is potential for rewiring and forming new connections, this could be why these effects are enduring and last long after the initial experience.

Many scientist believe DMT is produced from the pineal gland. Some scientist believe large amounts of DMT are released in the body at birth and death. The pineal gland also secretes melatonin which regulates sleep and wake cycles, and helps protect the body from free radicals. Some people can increase the amount of DMT their body naturally produces.

In some people DMT is released more doing meditation. It's also interesting that ancient cultures believed in the mystical and spiritual power of minds eye and knew about the pineal gland centuries ago. Ayahuasca is still viewed as a sacred plant in some cultures. The principal tryptamine found in ayahuasca is DMT. Some theorize that DMT is the chemical expression of a spiritual event, the entering or exiting of the spirit into a physical body.

The stories people tell after psychedelic experiences are often similar to people who claimed to have enlightenment experiences. Their view of reality is permanently altered. Common themes are a connectedness with everything, euphoria, hallucinations(or so they think), intense emotions, quieting of the mind, peace, and new understanding. It seems like that would be a stretch to say its a shared hallucination, especially if DMT is naturally occurring in our bodies and nature.

There have been some negative effects during usage of these drugs, yet I do believe the state of the mind prior to and during usage have a major affect on the outcome. You are still the master of your mind.

A chemical called Fluoride can cause calcification of the pineal gland. Fluoride is commonly found in tap water. Another coincidence if you believe in those.

DISCLAIMER
I am not recommending the use of psychedelics or any illegal substances. I am not recommending the recreational use of any potential dangerous substances. *DISCLAIMER*

I believe psychedelic substances should be studied more, they have great potential.

If psychedelics are indeed tools of consciousness, there is still another all natural tool that can be used obtain a deeper consciousness connection. That tool is called meditation.

10

Meditation

"Nowhere can man find a quieter or more untroubled retreat than in his own soul." ~Marcus Aurelius

I would describe a meditative state as achieving a state of consciousness different than your waking consciousness, where the barrier between the conscious mind, subconscious mind and all other forms of consciousness lessen. There are various meditative states in which you can connect with various forms of knowledge, power, healing, and creation. The meditative experience can be different for every practitioner.

Meditation is a tool used to quiet a noisy mind. Meditation is a tool that can show you the beauty and simplicity of existence. The proven benefits of meditation can include stress reduction, anxiety reduction, depression reduction, pain reduction, lengthening of attention spans, increased calmness, improved sleep, improved memory, and physical relaxation.

There are various meditation styles and techniques. If you wish to master your own mind you must enter your mind with that intent and find which methods work best for you.

I recommend studying Buddhism especially Buddhist meditation practices. Buddhist practitioners have been studying and honing meditation techniques for centuries. One of the primary goals of the Buddhist philosophy is achieving freedom from suffering. I believe many of the methods they use are effective and practical tools for reduction of suffering.

I offer a few practical tips that I use, and some notes from my own experiments.

I recommend finding a quiet location with few distractions, maintaining a comfortable posture, breathing from the diaphragm, and having a *focused* intention for your meditation session. I recommend closing your eyes or meditating in nature. Once you start meditating a good way to maintain this habit is to meditate at the same time and place. I recommend mediating after you wake up or before you slumber(when the barrier between conscious and subconscious is thin).

A technique to increase your *focus* is directed singular concentration. With this method you *focus* on a single concept, object or image. Usually something that is easy to visualize. You can *focus* on something internal or external. It can be as simple as a red circle, your heartbeat or your breathing. With this method you deliberately place your attention on the chosen object and maintain *focus* on that object for as long as possible. This practice helps strengthen your disciplined mind and can prolong your attention span. With this method you practice dismissing distractions, and enhance your ability to *focus*. Seasoned meditators can maintain this state for a few hours. The more you practice this method the quicker you will be able to notice when you are distracted, and you will learn how to recenter you *focus* quicker.

Directed singular concentration on your breathing is one of the easiest and most common meditation methods. Breathing is a subconscious process, so *focusing* on breathing is an effective way to bring your conscious attention to a subconscious process. You can *focus* on something external by keeping your eyes open and directing your *focus* on a specific object in your view. It can be anything, a flower, a painting, the ceiling or the ground. You may quickly begin to notice things that you often overlook and never took the time to examine and appreciate.

I recommend first person meditation for most practical meditations, especially for manifestation. First person meditation helps you become one with the reality your are visualizing. If you wish too manifest a new car, you can visualize your self inside the car, gripping the steering wheel, smelling the new car smell, adjusting the mirrors, and *focusing* on every small detail as if you're in that car. In your minds eye you must be in that car, experiencing reality in that car.

For pain reduction I frequently use a few methods. The first is deep concentrated *focus* on the area in pain, this can reduce the severity of the pain initially and when you return your *focus* to the rest of the body. Quieting of the mind and taking *focus* away from the body and self is another effective method. This helps by reminding your mind that you're not simply your body, you are a conscious being that is connected to a physical form, not simply a physical form.

One of the quickest and most simple relaxation techniques is just a few slow and deep breaths. This can be done anywhere to quickly recenter your *focus*.

For a slightly more advanced relaxation you can start by taking a few slow deep breaths. Then take a deep inhale and tense your whole body. Hold this breath and tension for five seconds, then release and exhale all of the air out of your body. Repeat this process three to five more times. After this technique you may feel instant relief and can conclude or use this as a getaway into another meditative practice.

For healing I use some guided meditations, and visualizations of the healthy body part functioning optimally. For extreme damage to the body I use a visualization method where I reconstruct the effected extremity, piece by piece until it is constructed perfectly. This method has been used by people for recovery from extreme injuries, like broken spinal cords, and paralysis. I also use various healing affirmations.

Too deeply connect with my body I do meditative body scans. I *focus* on breathing deeply, and breathing into the area where my current *focus* lies. I sometimes do body scans where I *focus* on the various chakra centers. This can free up energy, and help you notice if and where you have any blockages. Body massages and reiki massages are great tools to help connect with the body as well. Mixing these massages with concentrated meditative *focus* can help propel your meditation to new levels. Various soothing meditation sounds or frequencies can also increase the quality of your meditations.

For quieting of the mind/self/ego I practice resting awareness meditations, where I let my thoughts flow through my mind freely. I don't hold onto any thoughts, just observe them as an unbiased observer, and let them go as easily as they come. If I get distracted I return my *focus* onto my breathing, then slowly return my *focus* to nothingness. This method can help you realize that you can separate your emotions from your thoughts and that you can simply exist. When you can quiet the mind and dissolve the identity of self, you can achieve a form of enlightenment. In this method you can also use a noting technique where you can make mental notes of your thoughts and you can reassess your thoughts afterwards. Another method for quieting of the mind is a mantra mediation, you repeatedly say a mantra[7]. All of your *focus* is on saying the mantra, and eventually your *focus* can go to nothingness or deep state meditation.

Chakra meditations, and yoga meditations are great for stress relief, and connecting with the body. Be sure to take time for Shavasana, to relax the body and relieve tension. Resting awareness meditation is also great for stress relief.

A common thing people say who have survived prolonged periods of torture and maintained their sanity is that they create a mental safe space. They create a happy place and commit deep *focus* on that place. Mentally they go to their created place, and take their attention away from the physical body. Some people return to a positive memory, some create a vision of the future, and some create an imaginary place. In the mind you can go anywhere you desire, just build your reality and your mind will exist where your *focus* remains. In this method you enter a deep meditative state, and you escape the pain of your physical body.

These are just a few oversimplified methods that can benefit you in a variety of ways. Attempt a few if you are curious, and start your journey inward.

---

7   A phrase, word, or sound that is repeated by someone who is praying or meditating.

11

Empathy

Making everything personal is one of the highest forms of selfishness, because it makes the assumption that everything is centered around "you".

Once you stop making everything personal, you can begin to see everything as it is. Most anger comes from this selfishness.

Learning is essential, you must get to the point where you understand how minimal your perspective of reality is and then expand it. Empathy, understanding, and acceptance are often byproducts of this process. Empathy is not as common in this current reality as you may think. Sympathy is common because you can relate another experience to your own, it is easy because it is more selfish than empathy. True empathy is feeling the emotions and experiences of another person. That means not *focusing* on your reality but *focusing*, understanding and feeling their reality. That is true empathy, dissolving the self/ego/individual consciousness to experience and feel the reality of someone else(another consciousness).

"The true value of a human being is determined primarily by the measure and the sense in which he has attained to liberation from the self." ~Albert Einstein

I believe the truest and highest form of empathy is leaving your reality and experiencing another reality. Logically if you connect with one consciousness then you should be able to connect with all consciousness. That is a form of enlightenment. I would argue that empathy is naturally present in nearly all humans from birth, and if you have empathy you have a connection to all conscious entities.

It may seem mystical or spiritual but I would argue it is logical, but many modern sciences fail to take into account emotions and the power of the mind. If you believe empathy exist how do you disprove the idea of connected consciousness.

"A human being is a part of the whole, called by us 'Universe,' a part limited in time and space. He experiences himself, his thoughts and feelings as something separate from the rest — a kind of optical delusion of his consciousness. This delusion is a kind of prison for us, restricting us to our personal desires and to affection for a few persons nearest to us. Our task must be to free ourselves from this prison by widening our circle of compassion to embrace all living creatures and the whole of nature in its beauty." ~ Albert Einstein

Empathy is such a powerful emotion and experience because it opens to door to complete connection, understanding, and acceptance. With empathy you cannot deceive yourself into thinking you are any better or worse than someone else.

It appears that people who truly feel empathy seem to make impacts on humanity and the world. These people are sometimes wealthy, successful, loved, hated, misunderstood, but these people seem to succeed at whatever they set out to do. Does their consciousness connect to a collective consciousness. That might sound absurd, but we have already accepted scientifically that the universe/reality that we currently live in, can't exist without a connection to a conscious observer.

I believe that empathy is an emotion that harnesses great power through opening the door to a connected consciousness. Empathy is a gateway to connect individual conscious entities to a collective consciousness, and a collective consciousness may be the key to understand the entirety of the universe.

If you wish to practice and understand empathy better a good tool is method acting. When method actors find a role they fully immerse themselves into that role. Method actors try to study every aspect of the role they are playing. They study how the character thinks, what beliefs the character holds, what life circumstances lead to the characters current way of being, and everything else that they can deduce. Once they begin to understand the role/character, they begin to live as the new character. Method actors eat what food the character eats, follow the daily routine of the character, and interact with people as the character would. Method actors try to become the character or role they are playing. Method acting is an intense experience but a wonderful tool for expanding your perspective and becoming more empathetic.

12

Collective Consciousness Connection

"Never forget that the universe is a single living organism possessed of one substance and one soul, holding all things suspended in a single consciousness and creating all things with a single purpose that they might work together spinning and weaving and knotting whatever comes to pass."~Marcus Aurelius

A collective consciousness connection is the connection of multiple conscious entities. For the sake of simple understanding I will define THE CONSCIOUSNESS as the entirety of the universe, as one entity. THE CONSCIOUSNESS is sometimes referred to as, the ether, God, the universal force, the infinite intelligence, the living mind, the universal consciousness and many other names.

Awakening and interacting with this connection even momentarily is one form of enlightenment. You can achieve enlightenment with many world views, it is achievable through science, through love, through plenty of world religions and lifestyles. Enlightenment can be obtained by anyone.

The steps and tools I have mentioned in this book can simply make them easier. You must try for yourself and experiment with your reality. What you seek you shall find, you must simply seek it.

When you are enlightened through synchronization and synergy with THE CONSCIOUSNESS the entirety of your existence will make sense. Your vision becomes clear. Every action is directed towards a purpose. You will have access to the full power of the mind. You are connected with the full power of the universe. Every aspect of your life will have complete synchronization. You will begin too manifest quickly and easily. You will perform at the highest levels and attract people on similar frequencies. You will be able to truly live and appreciate your life to the fullest. You will see the true beauty of the human experience. You will regain the joy of a child, peace, bliss, and wisdom. You will begin to see how the universe communicates with you, and learn how to listen and benefit from this power.

Even if you don't believe in THE CONSCIOUSNESS, or haven't yet awakened into THE CONSCIOUSNESS, you can still connect with other conscious entities in various way.

Leonardo da Vinci believed that humans had an interconnectedness nature. He believed nearly everything that happens in the human body, resembles nature. This simple premise lead him to be one of the greatest artist, thinkers, inventors, and creators of his generation.

I agree with da Vinci and postulate that there is a conscious connection between nature and humanity as well. I believe that nature is a form of consciousness.

Nature provides us with sustenance, nourishment, cures for every ailment, plants with healing properties, and plants with chemicals that can help reach enlightenment and understanding of a shared consciousness connection. Nature is a constantly evolving conscious entity, that balances resources, population control, and effects the evolution of every species on earth.

Though it may be less common in societies today. Numerous ancient cultures knew the value of being connected with nature and living in harmony with nature. Connected consciousness arrangements lead to prosperity for all entities involved. Studies have shown that even minimal human connection with nature can lead to improved memory, increased happiness levels, pain reduction, increased concentration, increased vitamin D levels, immune system strengthening, and reduction of depression. These benefits can be received from simply spending a little time in nature, now imagine living in harmony with nature.

If you don't recognize nature as a conscious entity you can connect with the consciousness of other humans in a variety of ways.

There are countless stories of people having detailed visions and dreams, only to later find out that the visions did happen, and it was someone else's life experience that they had envisioned. Twins can often feel the emotions from the other twin. Some twins have shared thoughts, dreams and synchronized behaviors. These phenomenon are forms of a shared conscious connection.

There are numerous stories of people getting organ transplants which lead to visions, emotions, memories, and/or cravings from the initial owner of the organs. This phenomenon is known as cellular memory. Some organ transplants lead to complete personality changes. This phenomenon is similar to information being passed down through DNA. DNA is a highly advanced shared conscious connection. DNA consists of about 3 billion bases carrying information in different sequences. DNA shares conscious information between generations, and through millions of years of evolution. DNA communicates what information is needed to evolve and survive. DNA is all the proof you need of a shared consciousness connection. How else do you explain the dissemination of information through generations between entities that have never directly communicated. DNA transmits massive amounts of information directly into our subconscious minds. Also if you believe that all humans come from two people or one base DNA set, then you may conclude that there is some conscious connection between all humans simply through our connected DNA.

"The area where we are the greatest is the area in which we inspire, encourage and connect with another human being." ~Maya Angelou

I argue that the above statement is logical and not just something that people say. Evolution wired the human brain and body for empathy, logic, and yearning to feel connected to others, simply to propel the species further.

If you doubt that cooperation is a vital tool for the elevation of a species, then ponder for a second on why most species of animals don't cannibalize, or cant cannibalize without negative health effects. Evolution is one of the fundamental laws of the universe, and it sees the necessity for collaboration and mutually beneficial interaction between humanity.

If you don't believe you are a component of a shared consciousness connection, then ask yourself why you can feel someone looking at you. Why can you feel the energy from an energetic crowd. Why can you feel the pain in a sad song. We are all connected and if you want to awaken your awareness, you simply have to *focus* the mind on the conscious connection.

I believe that the next step in human evolution is a collective consciousness connection. Technology has evolved rapidly over the past 50 years yet the rate at which humans evolve is relatively slow. Evolution of the human body usually happens gradually and slowly over generations, but the limits of the mind are unknown. Every evolutionary adaptation for every species is intentional and direct towards overcoming some obstacle and propelling the species forward. The power of the mind, logic, reason, empathy, and emotions are all evolutionary adaptations so they are all necessary for the species to evolve.

I believe we have the tools required to intentionally and substantially direct the course of evolution. I believe the method that combines all of our evolutionary adaptations and aligns with the laws of the universe is a collective consciousness connection. Everything is connected through THE CONSCIOUSNESS, but that is not what I am referencing currently. I am referring to all of humanity in harmony tuning into a collective consciousness connection. If you have read the rest of this book, then you understand the power of this connection.

The path to a collective consciousness connection starts out which each individual striving to achieve enlightenment. The more people that achieve this the stronger the collective will become. Take control of yourself, to propel humanity forward. We are all one connected consciousness. We must dissolve the idea of the "them vs us". We are all one. The "them vs us" mentality is a sickness. This single idea has plagued humanity for far too long. As you start your journey and achieve this for yourself you must spread the word, and help others achieve inner peace and a connection with the collective.

One way humanity can work together to strengthen the collective consciousness connection is through shared meditation. A shared meditation will combine humanities shared *focus* and emotions and amplify the collective consciousness connection. I theorize that humanity achieving a shared collective consciousness connection may be easier to achieve than vast numbers of individuals connecting to THE CONSCIOUSNESS individually. I also theorize that once humanity achieves a collective consciousness connection it will be easier to connect and tap into THE CONSCIOUSNESS.

I propose that we come together and attempt a shared meditation with all humanity. If we use the shared power of humanities *focus*, emotions, and intent to achieve a collective consciousness connection I believe we can achieve it.

On Sunday September 9, 2029 at 5:00pm CST,

I plan to attempt a shared meditation with humanity. I hope you will join me and try to propel humanity towards the next step in evolution. I believe THE CONSCIOUSNESS is present and will always be present, but I believe a worldwide shared meditation attempt is the way the masses can connect to this power, and the whole of humanity can start to harness this power. For this attempt I encourage you to simply to meditate at the stated time with the intent to connect and resonate with all of humanity.

Until humanity achieves a collective consciousness connection you can *focus* on controlling the conscious entities you keep around yourself.

13

Company

The people surrounding you can have a major impact on your life. Your income is usually an average of the five people closest to you. Emotions are contagious, unconscious motor mimicry can lead you to feel the emotions of people around you. Mindsets and beliefs are also contagious, so asses how people think before you devote your time and energy towards them.

Remember we are beings made up of energy, so if you wish to live on a certain frequency then you should surround yourself with more of the same frequency. If you constantly interact with opposing frequencies it is only logical that your frequency will change. Control your surroundings or they will begin to control you.

If you surround yourself with like minded people, success at achieving goals becomes easier. Most of human innovation has come from collaboration. One individual conscious entity can achieve great things, but a collective conscious-ness working harmoniously towards a goal creates synergy, unlocking the highest levels of achievement. Teamwork makes dreams work.

Having deep meaningful connection with others helps dissolve the ego, and we know dissolving the ego is essential in achieving various form of enlightenment.

You should find good people and create a support system for yourself. You should surround yourself with people that inspire you, and who bring positivity, happiness, and love into your life. If you have trouble finding such people first remove people who drain you, limit you, and bring negativity in your life. Once you stop tolerating what doesn't belong in your life you will have space to evolve and attract what you desire in your life.

Good company can also give you various perspectives that you don't always see yourself. Perspective is key in understand and expanding your current way of thinking. Be cautious of all proven liars or people with a poor relationship with objectivity and objective truths. These people are dangerous in any capacity.

Many people have troubles with relationships for a variety of reason. I propose this simple fix that may solve many issues. Write down everything you're looking for in your relationships and that you desire from other people. **SKIP THE REST OF THIS PARAGRAPH UNTIL AFTER YOU FINISH YOUR LIST!!!!!!!!!!!!!!!!!!!!! GO TO THE NEXT PARAGRAPH AND RESUME READING. (FOLLOW INSTRUCTIONS FOR MAXIMUM EFFECTIVENESS)(MARK THIS PLACE IN THE BOOK)** Once you have finished your list, work to become everything on that list for yourself. In the process of becoming what you are looking for you will mostly likely attract more of the same or realize you already have everything that you need.

In the company you keep you should always have at least one mentor. Wisdom is valuable and will make life much easier. If you don't know anyone with the knowledge you seek, learn as I did, from wise people through reading. Nearly every problem humans encounter has been solved practically, theoretically, or scientifically and the knowledge is readily available and easily accessible. Seek and use this wisdom and you will overcome centuries of evolutionary struggle.

Assess your current company, and make the necessary adjustments. Devote time and effort into choosing the correct people to surround yourself with. A few moments of consideration can alter the course of your life. Understand the magnitude your surroundings have on your fate and choose wisely.

14

Practical Applications

- Add variety to routines to combat stagnation and boredom
- Use worst case consequence analysis and weighted average decision matrices or other logical and analytically tools for difficult decisions. If you have a logical basis for decision making you can tame your emotions in a difficult situations, and think with a clear mind.
- Use an accountability partner
- Master a fundamental pillar of discipline, control what you eat.
- **Write the list from the COMPANY chapter, then return there instructions.**
- Have mentors
- Adopt a growth mindset
- Collaborate with like minded people
- Remove self limiting ideas, thoughts and beliefs
- Believe that anything is possible
- Teach children to think and how to think
- Don't limit kids minds, they are naturally creative curious philosophers
- When you set a goal ponder how you can achieve 10x that goal. You will see how much easier doing it once is
- Read and learn for at least one hour a day (listen in the car to not effect daily routines)
- Ask the thinking questions (why and how)

- Pause momentarily and think before you respond
- Listen to comprehend, and not just to respond
- Directly ask the question you want answered (This is better for all parties involved)
- Choose your words carefully. Communication is how you express to the world who you are
- Track and quantify your results(Most people are delusional about their reality)
- Meditate
- Shared meditation
- Discover your primary purpose
- Take actions directed towards your primary purpose daily
- Set achievable daily goals, and always complete the task you set for yourself.
- Seek and value criticism, strive to strengthen your weaknesses
- Remove "can't" from your vocabulary.
- Write down ideas that pop into your head.
- Write down your dreams.
- Make your subconscious mind work for you.
- Make sure your last thoughts before bed are positive
- Wake up on the first alarm
- Start your day off by making your bed (This is a psychological trick that starts your day by completing a task. This tip is so effective it has been adopted by the military)
- Speak affirmations to yourself
- Vision Board
- Get outside of your comfort zone at least once daily (1 minute cold shower)
- Stand up, and move around (humans are not designed to be sedentary for 13+ hours a day)
- Find a diet that optimizes your performance
- Take vitamins. (Most people are deficient in something, either genetically or due to poor diet)
- 60-90 minute sessions of deep *focused* work

- Temporarily limit one or more of your senses to aid with deep *focus* (noise canceling headphones)
- Dopamine Detox
- Apply the concepts and tools learned from this book into your daily life(learning is important but application is essential)
- Consciously *focus* on appreciating life, the habitual routines, the mundane activities, the minute details, and the beauty of existence. Try to appreciate life as a neanderthal would if he were placed in our society.

Epilogue

The main reason I wrote this book is to spread knowledge and to attempt to push humanity towards the next steps of evolution. To this end

On Sunday September 9, 2029 at 5:00pm CST, I will attempt a shared meditation with humanity. I hope you will join me in, and try to propel humanity towards the next step in evolution. The key to achieving this goal is to spread this information, and continue learning about the power within ourselves.

There has always been great wisdom in the world the key is to share the information with the masses. Spread the information, debate, disprove faulty premises, learn and evolve.

It has brought me great pleasure to study these concepts, to learn from the visionaries of the past, to think and to formulate my own opinions. Even if you do not agree with any or all of my thoughts, I encourage you to pursue truth. I thank you for reading my book and supporting me through purchasing one of my life's work.

If my book has added some value to your life, please send out some positive energy towards me, and please put more positive energy into the universe. Please share this information with others and refer this book to anyone you feel needs or wants this information.

I hope this book has inspired you to study humans and explore the power of creation. The past and present are full of people who are using parts of this ability to alter the course of humanity. The next person to tap into this power could be you.

Appendix 2

Logical arguments against the majority of pre-established religions.

Which interpretation(of the religion/philosophy and the accompany text)- Often people and religious institutions interpret the text in a way that benefits the current objective. A quick study of history can prove this. If the interpretation varies easily how close is your application of the religion to the original principles.

Translation- Many religious text have been translated numerous times between numerous languages. There is nearly always error when translating because of the variability of how languages were designed. Many languages have words to describe concepts that aren't relevant in other cultures or languages. Multiple seemingly small errors in communication lead to massive misapplication of fundamental principles. This alone leads to multiple branches of religions being formed. Do you believe all of the translators adequately understood the text, and were competent in their abilities to translate. Do you know who translated the text? Are their words or concepts used in your current translation that didn't exist at the origin of the text? Can you deduce the original language that the text was created in and read it in that language?

Intentional Alteration- Did the people who maintained and translated the text intentionally alter the text to achieve a certain goal? Is it likely that people altered it for political power, financial gain, or to pursue their desires? Many people know the massive power religions have had on the direction of human society. Religious text are often the bestselling book in a society. Do you know who maintained and monitored the authenticity of the text?

Original Text- Can you trace back the linage of the text and verify the details with any certainty? Do you know where the current text or version of your philosophy is derived from?

Text Written by Humans- Many religions have prophets or people who receive the message and interpret it. The problem with human interpretation is that it we all receive information differently, perceive reality differently, and process information differently. If two prophets receive the same vision, they will interpret and explain it differently. Which can lead to errors in the original formation of the text. Any slight variation from the objective truth can lead to horrible practical misapplications of the doctrine.

Informed Decision- Have your thoroughly read and studied your religion/philosophy and believe you deeply understand it. Do you think that your religion/philosophy adequately describes the laws of the universe and/or aligns with it. Have you factored in the arguments stated above. Have you thoroughly studied other religions/philosophies to verify that yours is the objective truth or the closest to the objective truth?

www.ingramcontent.com/pod-product-compliance
Lightning Source LLC
Chambersburg PA
CBHW021211020426
42331CB00003B/310